HEMP

AN INCREDIBLE STORY

Matteo Gracis is an Independent journalist and free thinker. He is the Founder and Director of alternative lifestyle magazine "Dolce Vita". He's served as a Communications Advisor in Italian Parliament. He's an expert on the culture of hemp, and has consulted some of the most prominent European companies in the field.

Also by Free Mind Publications

This is not Leonardo da Vinci – Riccardo Magnani

MATTEO GRACIS

HEMP

AN INCREDIBLE STORY

Translated from the Italian by Free Mind Publications

Free Mind Publications

First published in Italian as *Canapa, una storia incredibile,* April 2019

Cover chart project: Samuel Re

Cover photo: Fabio Baggio

Editing by Carmen Laterza and Francesca D'Ancona

Contribution of historical research: Andrea Legni

www.matteogracis.it

copyright 2020 Chinaski S.r.l.

All rights reserved

Officina di Hank is a brand run by Chinaski S.r.l.

English language edition 1.

English language edition copyright © 2021 Free Mind Publications.

ISBN: 978-0-6450675-3-8 (trade paper edition)

ISBN: 978-0-6450675-2-1 (ebook)

They tried to bury us.

They didn't know we were seeds.

Dinos Christianopoulos

Contents

Preface 7
Her Majesty the Hemp 9
A Distant History 13
Rebel youth 23
The near miss revolution 31
Ghosts and the community 37
Witch Hunt 49
Dolce Vita 61
War on drugs 71
You reap what you sow 79
What about in Italy? 89
Counterinformation and truth 101
She heals 113
Life is a journey 125
The new era 133
Hemp won 139
A green future 149
Dad, what is Hemp? 157
Afterword 159
Glossary 161
Bibliography 165

PREFACE

> *Spliff yes or spliff no? It's a stupid question. The big question is: what happened to Hemp? How can a plant be outlawed? We outlawed a plant. Because of one of its dumbest uses. Smoking it is one of the dumbest uses. It's like you drink, you get some cirrhosis, and we outlaw the vineyard!*

So began my monologue during a show of mine in '97. I was accused by everyone just for having used the term spliff. Since then I have never censored myself, as I never did after all.

When I received Matteo's book (in my opinion one of the most complete about Hemp), I could only enhance his commitment and support him in one of the most controversial battles of our Country - Italy.

These are the great battles to fight for, which can shake up cosmic economic interests and change the lives of each of us.

This is politics, you do it outside the Palace, in the pages of this book, where Matteo takes us in a fascinating world, unknown to most, through stories, anecdotes, and places. He does it with his crazy life, his work and his magazine.

Congratulations, then, to this young writer who tells us about the Hemp world with passion, competence and curiosity.

Read it and spread the word!

Long live Hemp!

Beppe Grillo

Hemp, an incredible story

Chapter 1

HER MAJESTY THE HEMP

From Nang, Vietnam. 1997. I'm fourteen years old and I'm traveling with my parents. A holiday on the road, north to south, from Hanoi to Ho Chi Minh. Two weeks on ramshackle coaches crossing that slice of Southeast of Asia nestled in the jungle. A great experience, like any of those off the beaten track.

My parents are experienced travelers, and they know how to move around the world. This skill is certainly the most precious legacy that they have left to me.

They hear about a particular excursion, a one-day boat trip that must be done, "you have to see it, to believe it". And there we go; we book the trip in the small office of a local tour operator and the next morning we leave. We're onboard, a classic group tour boat, everybody anonymously spread across twelve to thirteen meters of space across two floors. There are about thirty of us, many American tourists, some Australians and a few Europeans. The average age is thirty-something - I'm the only teenager. The staff consists of six members. Lady Mama is the Captain, a short and stout old lady, a little ambiguous and forcibly sympathetic, dispensing great smiles to the guests.

With blue sky above and a few waves, we leave the small port towards the open sea, the South China Sea.

After an abundant hour of navigation, we approach a beautiful inlet with crystal clear water and rocks overlooking the sea. Lady Mama shouts orders at sailors who run on the deck. They drop anchor, and everybody excitedly dives into the water for a dip.

A few minutes later, Lady Mama also enters the water, supported by a float, pushing before her a distinctive pop-corn tray. She slowly approaches a tourist, takes a glass jar from the tray, extracts a strange cigarette - bigger than normal - passes it to the tourist and lights it for him. The guy greedily inhales and soon after, a thirty-two teeth smile appears on his face. He splashes in the turquoise sea, under the sun, holding – what I will later discover to be – a joint of amazing weed. He is in heaven.

Lady Mama meanwhile continues the tour and supplies all the bathing guests the same way, which they all greatly appreciate. Together with the joint[1], everyone is also offered a glass of fresh sangria. In a few minutes the situation is surreal, amid irrepressible laughter and a collective euphoria seemingly out of control... but not dangerous at all. In the meantime, in fact, the staff members launched life jackets to their colleagues in the water, prudently given to the most stoned among the swimmers. Some abandon themselves to the mercy of slight waves and hallucinations. When one floats too far from the boat, Lady Mama sends one of her staff to recover the "dispersed" person; and she almost seems pleased to have this absolute control on her passengers, especially the Americans.

Is it just an impression of mine or does her enjoyment stem from the long dragging of an old war never forgotten? Who can tell?

The fact is that in all this my parents wonder – amused, but still apprehensive –how to hide or explain to me this mini-Woodstock 2.0.

Once back on board, on the roof-terrace of the boat, we are welcomed with an amazing exotic fruit buffet, fresh and exquisite. A triumph of colors!

In the midst of the Vietnamese sea, in scorching heat and falling prey to the "munchies"[2], the gringos have ecstatic expressions and the light I see shining in their eyes looks like that of those who have reached nirvana.

And here the word of mouth that came to us of a special trip was explained, not to be missed, "you have to see it to believe it". Lady Mama has found a combination of services that can offer a unique and unforgettable experience to its guests.

---

[1] Made of pure marijuana, without tobacco.
[2] Sudden hunger that often follows the consumption of Cannabis

I don't actually experience anything, my parents keep me at a proper distance from Lady Mama's "special" services, but I look around and understand. Or, rather, I grasp something.

But what I still do not know -- and that right now I cannot even imagine – is how important she will become to me from few years later, how much space she will take up in my life, how much longer she will remain by my side, albeit in gradually different ways.

She, her majesty, the Hemp.

Hemp, an incredible story

Chapter 2

A Distant History

Qufu, China. 2737 B.C.E

Among the fertile land surrounding the ancient capital, the Emperor Shen Nung studied and experimented with new agricultural techniques and innovative medical preparations. Local myths still celebrate him today as a divine farmer and healer. He is credited with the composition Shen Nung Ben Ts' ao, the body of knowledge upon which millennia of traditional Chinese medicine is based. It contains more than three hundred natural elements with therapeutic properties. Among them, cannabis occupies a place of honor.

Each part of the plant is examined and studied in the book. The flowers, prepared in a tisane, are recommended to treat rheumatic disorders pains, intestinal constipation, gynecological disorders, malaria and headache. The seeds serve to counteract dysmenorrhea, indigestion, intestinal weakness, vomiting, intoxication and diarrhea. For skin diseases, ulcers and wounds, its oil is used instead. Referencing the bases of Shen Nung and the earliest pharmacopeial writings, Chinese doctors for centuries used high doses of cannabis inflorescences in the preparation of anesthetics to be administered before surgeries[3]. Even today the Chinese word "anesthesia" is made by two characters - 麻醉 - respectively meaning "cannabis" and "intoxication".

Palos de la Frontera, Spain. 3 August 1492.

Christopher Columbus was about to set sail, commanding ninety sailors arranged on three ships renamed the Niña, the Pinta and the Santa Maria. After years of spasmodic fundraising, finally everything was predisposed to leave for India – so he believed –through a route never tried before, the western one. The Navigator from Genova was already tasting fame, wealth and the possibility of becoming viceroy of all the

---

3 Grotenhermen F., Huppertz R., *Cannabis as medicine.*

new lands, but he knew well that he first had to sagely cross the Atlantic Ocean. In short, glory or death: there were no middle ways.

For this reason, nothing could go wrong. The three caravels had to be ready to face a journey of weeks, through seas never furrowed, they had to be indestructible and maneuverable at the same time. The sails would face the impetus of the strongest winds, ready to drag boats of more than a hundred tons. The ropes that controlled them had to withstand the corrosive action of salt water. Manufacturers did not have any doubts about the material to use: all ropes, cables and sails were entirely made of Hemp fiber[4]. Nothing –the artisans of the time stated – was more robust and elastic at the same time. But that's not all, Hemp was also present on board: the oil from its seeds served to operate the lamps, indispensable for consulting maps at night. On October 12, all three caravels docked on the coast of El Salvador. They made it. Thanks to her, the Hemp, the exploration of what then turned out be America, began.

New York, United States. February 24, 1794.

George Washington was in his second term and in the meantime, he continued to take care of the five family farms. The first President of the United States sent a letter to the director who ran the estates in his absence: "I am very glad to hear that the gardener has saved so much Indian Hemp seeds," he wrote, "let the ground be well prepared. Hemp may be sown anywhere"[5].

Thomas Jefferson too, the third President of the United States, was an agricultural entrepreneur and he also believed the cultivation of Hemp was so important that he personally engaged in the construction of the first machine capable of mechanically separating the fibers. That's not all: to improve the quality of his crops, Jefferson improvised himself as a smuggler. While he was in France in his role as Ambassador – between

---

4 Ciano C., Gay F., *The Ships of Christopher Columbus*, Polygraphy Institute and Mint of the State, 1992.

5 Washington G., The writings of George Washington, vol. 12, Worthington Chauncey Ford, 1989.

1784 and 1789 – he involved his agents in order to transport a batch of valuable seeds from China and illegally arrived in Paris through Turkey[6].

In his diaries he annotated:

> *The best Hemp and the best tobacco grow on the same kind of soil. The former is of first necessity to the commerce and marine, in other words to the wealth and protection of the country, the latter never useful, and sometimes pernicious derives its Estimation from Caprice, and its Value from the Taxes to which it was formerly exposed. Hemp employs in its rudest State more Labor than Tobacco, but being a Material for Manufactures of various Sorts becomes afterwards the Means of Support to Numbers of People hence it is to be preferred in a populous Country[7].*

Here then are three stories of distant eras from opposite latitudes, demonstrating how She, Hemp, has accompanied the life of mankind in practically every era and place, as source of sustenance and food, as a medicine, as an essential raw material, and as a fundamental ingredient for mystical experiences and rituals.

However, no one in past centuries has thought of the necessity to create arbitrary and unjustified distinctions between Hemp and marijuana, i.e. the varieties with a low and high THC content, tetrahydrocannabinol, the active ingredient of cannabis. The former, with low THC content, is more suitable for industrial use, while the latter, those with a high content of THC, is instead capable of causing psychotropic effects. Obviously from a botanical point of view it's a nonsensical distinction, yet capable of causing catastrophe.

Cannabis has therefore been present in the world for about fifteen thousand years. Where from and how it has spread is still a topic of debate among scholars. For a long time it was believed that the first strain grew in Central Asia around 12,000 B.C.E., in a region stretching from northwest of the Himalayas to China, and then spread, through

---

[6] Herer J., *The Emperor wears no clothes*, Ah Ha Publishing, 1985.
[7] Bröckers M., Herer J., *Hemp*, Parole di Cotone Edizioni, 1999.

migrations, to the rest of the world four thousand years ago. The most recent analyses, however, has cast doubt on this thesis, demonstrating how Hemp was present in Europe in its wild status almost in parallel with the first Asian strains. At present, the most ancient traces of its presence in the old continent have been found in Italy, near Lake Abano, in the province of Rome, and date back to 11,500 BCE.[8]

Whatever the truth is, it is a fact that it has been spread for thousands of years practically all over the planet, including those latitudes where very few vegetable species can thrive. Nature has in fact gifted her with the ability to adapt to each climate, perfecting three main varieties:

- Cannabis indica, up to five meters high and above, originally from Asia and spread around all sub-tropical areas.
- Cannabis sativa, lowest and thickest, present in Europe, Africa and tropical areas of America and Asia.
- Cannabis ruderalis, of bush-like shape, capable to live and thrive wildly in the harshest climates of Russia and northern China.

And wherever she grew, man soon understood her infinite properties.

On a therapeutic level, the knowledge of the ancient Chinese pharmacy soon spread far beyond the confines of the celestial empire, becoming part of the traditional pharmacopoeias of half of the world. The Assyrians used it to fight depression, arthritis, kidney stones, menstrual pain and impotence, while with her oil they prepared ointments to rub on bruises and swelling.

In the Arabian Peninsula she was first used against convulsions, in the treatment of a probable epileptic syndrome[9]. It was 1464, over five centuries before the benefits of THC in the treatment of this disease was confirmed by Western medicine.

---

[8] Samorini G., *14,000 years of Italian Hemp*, www.dolcevitaonline.it, 2017.

[9] Mathre M., *Cannabis in medical practice*, Mc Farland, 1997.

A Distant History

But the region where Hemp was studied and used more than anywhere else was India. Here, for a thousand years before Christ, she was used to treat a hundred affections: Indian doctors added new usages to the already known ones, with analgesic purposes, anticonvulsants, anti-inflammatories, antibiotics and against bronchitis, asthma and loss of appetite. The properties of cannabinoids[10] were also used on the psyche as an aphrodisiac, hypnotic, and tranquilizer. Ancient Indian science on Cannabis was so precise and specialized that it had put in place three types of preparations, which exploited the different parts of the plant to best treat every disorder:

- the *Bhang*, consisting only of dried leaves.
- the *Ganja*, prepared with flowers.
- the *Charas*, the strongest and psychoactive compound, made exclusively with the resins that cover the inflows.

From India, in more recent times, the knowledge of cannabis as a drug arrived in Europe and then, to the United States. Its pioneer was an Irish doctor named William Brooke O'Shaughnessy who in the 1930s – being of service in India –studied her uses for therapeutic purposes, becoming so impressed that he decided to devote himself to the experimentation of these treatments on his own patients. Once back home in 1939, he wrote the first medical manual dedicated to cannabinoids, describing the successes achieved in treating rheumatism, convulsions and spasms due to tetanus and rabies[11].

At the same time, the French psychiatrist Jacques Moreau, after a trip to Morocco, began testing cannabis in the treatment of some

---

[10] To date, one hundred and twenty active ingredients called Cannabinoids have been identified in Cannabis. Their distribution varies in the different Cannabis strains and in general only three or four cannabinoids are found in a plant with a concentration higher than 0.1%. The best known are THC (tetrahydrocannabinol) and CBD (cannabidiol), responsible for many of its medicinal virtues, but research is now concentrating also on other cannabinoids such as CBC (cannabichromene), which is believed to have large antibacterial and anti-inflammatory properties.

[11] Mikuriya T., *Marijuana in medicine: past, present and future*, Calif Med, 1969

psychiatric patients in his Parisian study. In this case the results were so encouraging that they convinced him to write an essay to share his discoveries with the European scientific community.

The impact of O'Shaughnessy and Moreau's trials on Western medicine of the time was resounding; and more trials started all over Europe and then in the universities of North America.

In 1860, the first world conference on medical cannabis was held in Ohio, and in the second half of the 19th century, the scientific articles published on the subject were more than one hundred worldwide[12].

Western medicine thus discovered cannabis and it can be said – without exaggeration – that it was largely revolutionized, while pharmaceutical companies began to develop and distribute the first medicines based on it.

Cannabis thus entered the official pharmacopoeia of every state, and every year dozens of ships sailed from India to Western ports laden with inflorescences ready to be transformed and traded mainly in the form of oils and syrups, but also as cigarettes already rolled – with names such as Cannabin Bell, Neem Tail and Miracle Elixir – on whose packaging cannabinoids were defined as the "instant remedy against many afflictions".

Cannabis-based remedies were advertised in newspapers and magazines. On 4 October 1862, in the weekly magazine Vanity Fair, the advertising of hashish-based candies appeared, defining them as "A most wonderful Medicinal Agent for the cure of Nervousness. Weakness. Melancholy. Confusion of thoughts, etc. A pleasurable and harmless stimulant"[13].

The afflictions against which cannabinoids were regularly prescribed were many. The Analytical Cyclopedia of Practical Medicine published in 1924 recommended them for insomnia, senile insomnia, melancholy, delirium tremens, chorea, tetanus, rabies, allergic rhinitis, bronchitis, pulmonary tuberculosis, cough, Parkinson's, Grave's disease, bladder

---

[12] Grinspoon L., *Marijuana reconsidered*, Harvard University Press, 1971.

[13] *Vanity Fair*, no. 145, 4 October 1862

spasms, gonorrhea, headache, migraine, eye fatigue, menopause, brain tumor, neuralgia, gastric ulcer, indigestion, neuropathies, uterus disorders, dysmenorrhea, chronic inflammation, menorrhagia, abortion threats, post-partum hemorrhage, rheumatism, eczema, senile itching, tingling, dental pain relief, lack of appetite, anorexia, gastric neurosis, dyspepsia, diarrhea, dysentery, cholera, nephritis, hematuria, diabetes mellitus, heart palpitations, dizziness, female sexual atonia and male impotence[14].

Many people have, at various times, renamed Hemp the 'magic plant' or the 'miraculous plant'. In our modern and rational eyes these might seem like exaggerated definitions, but for sure we can call it the 'unique plant'. It is a fact that its different parts have been vital to every civilization for three main reasons: they guarantee food, heal, and constitute a raw material. Not for nothing did Hemp earn the nickname "vegetable pig": as in the case of pigs, you do not throw anything away from it.

If flowers and oil were fundamental ingredients for medicine, the plant's stalk has been for millennia the main material for construction. It is composed of two parts: the bast fiber, used for the manufacturing of ropes, yarns and fabrics of all kinds, and the hurd, that is, the woody part inside the external layer, for centuries an excellent raw material for the production of every type of paper, as well as fuel for domestic hearths, due to its low humidity and ability to burn slowly, releasing much heat before flaming out.

As for the medical uses of the flower, even the cannabis stalk's multifaceted qualities have been known since ancient times. From 1,000 B.C.E. until after the Industrial Revolution, Hemp represented the most important element for every industry in a large part of the world[15]. For what reason? Simply because in nature there is no fiber that is stronger, longer lasting and more durable.

In the botanical world, Hemp is in fact unique. It has an annual life cycle but does not impoverish the soil, to the point that it does not need – this is more unique than rare – rotation. In a single season it develops

---

[14] Mathre M., *Cannabis in medical practice,* Op. Cit.
[15] Herer J., *The Emperor wears no clothes* Op. Cit.

woody stalks three to six meters high, ensuring, in warmer latitudes, more than one annual harvest. It can be grown with good results even on less fertile soils and ensures a high quantity of product per hectare, not needing more than a few inches of space between plants in crops for textile purposes. No other plant in nature possesses these qualities all together!

90% of naval sails from the Phoenician era to the end of the nineteenth century – that is until the mass spread of steamboats – were made of Hemp fiber[16], and so too all the cordage, fishing nets and protective covers to prevent wood erosion. The same applies to clothing which has warmed and protected generations of men, including the first working model of the legendary Levi's jeans, produced in the mid-19th century with Hemp fiber pockets, the only material capable of not tearing under the weight of nuggets collected by gold panners.

Since the first sheets conceived in China over 2,000 years ago, and then in Arab countries, Europe and the United States, paper too was produced, for much of human history, mainly thanks to Hemp. The first printed book in Europe, the famous Gutenberg Bible of 1453, was made on Hemp paper, as well as, over three centuries later, were written the drafts of the Declaration of Independence of the United States of America, a country in which even the first specimens of the national flag were made of Hemp fiber.

Hemp-made were the canvases used by Van Gogh, Rembrandt and many other painters; canvases that resisted the erosion of time, mold and light thanks to the extraordinary strength of Hemp fiber. The lamps that illuminated the night in the four corners of the world used the oil of her seeds. Seeds that have been used as an extraordinarily nutritious and economical ingredient for flours and soups that have fed millions of farmers in the past, often saving them from famine.

---

[16] Abel E., *Marijuana: the first 12000 years*, Plenum Press, 1980.

A Distant History

And when the fortuitous invention of champagne made it necessary to introduce cages to keep the caps in place against the push of the bubbles, braided threads of Hemp were used to make them[17].

The list could go on forever, but... the concept is clear: Hemp was everywhere.

By now then it should no longer come as a surprise her definition as "the Means of Support to Numbers of People, hence it is to be preferred in a populous Country" by Thomas Jefferson. As in the whole world so in the United States, Hemp has long been a farming of strategic importance, difficult to understand with our modern eyes. But the peculiar history of the States is useful to add one last tile to the forgotten past of this plant.

For a long time the United States, unlike other countries, had insufficient Hemp production to cover the needs of the mighty advancement of its capitalism. American industries were forced to import it from abroad, a circumstance that was considered a serious obstacle to the economic development of the country, so much so that special laws to promote their cultivation, sometimes even coercively, were implemented in various states. As an example, in 1619 the Virginian state government promulgated a law that ordered all land holders to allocate part of the plots to the sowing of Hemp. Similar measures were taken in the following years in Massachusetts and Connecticut. It went on like this for decades, with further crackdowns in times of the greatest shortage of raw materials, as between 1763 and 1767, when in Virginia the non-compliance with the law on the cultivation of the plant became even a criminal offence subject to arrest[18].

That's right: there was a time when those who risked to ending up in prison for cannabis was not those who cultivated it, but those who refused to do it!

---

[17] Michel Grilliat, *The Tools of Champagne*, Dominique Fradet Editions - 1998

[18] Herndon G.M., *Hemp in colonial Virginia*, Agricultural History Review, 1963.

Chapter 3

REBEL YOUTH

A few years after the experience in Vietnam on Lady Mama's boat, I find myself at the turn of the new millennium with a terrible character, a punchable face, a desire to fistfight the whole world. I am a classic sixteen-year-old know-it-all, with the truth in my pocket and the music up loud on my Walkman, so as to ensure any well-intentioned advice keeps its distance.

In the meantime, even in the small mountain village where I was born and bred, the first drunken nights arrive, the parties at my friends' house, and Saturday nights spiced up by alcohol and tobacco.

We drank much - often too much - and without discernment. Mixing beer, wine, grappa, vodka, Baileys, Montenegro, Jägermeister, and so on. Sometimes you throw up, other times you don't; but in that case it's even worse, because the poison stays in your stomach and at night the bed spins like a whirlpool.

Then one night at a party, someone pulls out something different from the usual – rumors say it's natural, almost harmless – they say it makes you laugh; but mainly it represents transgression, and that's what got our attention. La Marijuana. Here she was!

Filter, long rolling paper, tobacco from half a cigarette mixed with weed... and we roll the ugliest doob in history. But who cares?

'Come on, light it up!'

We smoke, curious to feel the effects. The first inhale is always a placebo, but after the second toke, you already see dragons and fireworks in the sky. After a few minutes, the real effects arise, and we laughed out loud, confronting our reactions. Bent over with laugher, our thoughts get light, someone mumbles something incomprehensible... and the laughing resumes. What a blast! That's her, the mythical Mary Jane.

For some of us – I being one of them – it was tantamount to the discovery of America. For others, it was the devil. Not my problem, we smoke and you laugh. Fuck the rest.

Red eyes? Eye drops.

"What if they catch us?" We hide.

"Is Mary Jane over!" We get some pot.

"Is pot over too?" We grow weed.

In the meantime, in between spliffs, I am in the midst of a teenage crisis and as I turn seventeen, I write down in my diary:

> I'm afraid to grow up. I'm afraid of just existing, when I would like to live, at least a thousand times. I'm nostalgic for the present, have no remorse for the past and a fucking fear of the future.
>
> In the end, the existence that each of us leads is as useless as it is boring - it is insignificant, it is based on work, on the conflict for a continuous and spontaneous challenge with others, on what our eyes see more easily and sometimes (in luckier cases) on some little, often forbidden, vice. Man seems great to me if he can invent a god, a moral, a conscience, a paradise and a hell. Any credible and solid motivation to give at the same time, in every corner of the earth - hope, faith, mercy, tolerance, the desire to live, to get up, to continue.

However, alternate moments of euphoria and important carefree reflections mixed with discomfort remain ignored by me – I pay them no attention, or time. I get high and put existential doubts under the carpet.

My school career is turbulent to say the least and I end up in a boarding school in Feltre, the second biggest city in the province of Belluno. Here, more than devoting myself to the study of traditional subjects, my attention goes to my female schoolmates, but above all to the discovery of new techniques for cannabis cultivation out-door and indoor.

I then throw myself into something I like and so my very first editorial project is born, a fanzine dedicated to hip hop culture titled

Styloso. Only two issues come out and it's a total fiasco, especially from an economic point of view. In reality though, for the future, the initiative will reveal itself as very useful and formative.

Unsurprising I fail at school – disappointing my parents – but I come back home loaded with interesting experiences.

So begins my lowlife period, with nights out in search of trouble and psycho-physical alteration. We go hitchhiking and one night the SUV in which I sit goes off the road and crashes into the only pole that prevents it flying down a cliff. I come out miraculously unharmed.

These are the first years of the 2000s, in which I turn eighteen and the first driving licenses among the friends arrive, as do the first mobile phones.

Hollywood churns out a film that inevitably attracts our attention and, laying on the sofa with a joint in hand and ten butts already put out in the ashtray, we listen in trance to a key quote: "Well, in all honesty, I don't feel that what I've done is a crime. I think it's illogical and irresponsible for you to sentence me to prison. Because, when you think about it, what did I really do? I crossed an imaginary line with a bunch of plants...."

We have shivers and shiny eyes. Blow plays on a loop for some months and George Jung, also known as Boston George, masterfully played by Johnny Depp, quickly replaces the childhood hero on the wall of my bedroom.

We buy weed or pot, a few grams at a time, from a group of guys a few years older than us, who clearly skim on every gram. We practically pay gold for every spliff. A real tragedy for our empty pockets at the time. So we eventually decide to skip these intermediaries by sourcing what we need directly from the city, and we organize the first stocking trips. Three-to-four hundred kilometers at a time for a few dozen grams, which soon become hundreds. We make the whip-round between friends to gather the necessary amount. The goal of the trip is to repay the expenses and fulfill our own needs: in short, we aim to smoke for free. There is no speculative intent. But the risk we run is very high, and we naturally faced it with the superficiality typical of our age. If it is true that in your teens everyone does some stunts, we outdid our peers tenfold without realizing.

Idiots!

Within a few months demand increased and so too did the amount of substance handled. We buy the first kilos. Albanian weed of very low quality - full of seeds - but it's cheap and potent, so everybody likes it. By buying by the kilo, we pay three thousand lire per gram and sell it at a markup twice or three times the cost. We move a lot of it and for a while groups of friends from all over the province and beyond come to get their supply from us.

One of those evenings I'm in Bologna, at a party in a community center, when someone close to me starts rolling a doob while he chats.

"This is not great, I got it from a friend from Belluno, but we're in a shortage period and there is nothing else around."

The doob goes around and eventually comes to me, I take a toke and recognize instantly that disgustingly unmistakable taste. I'm smoking "my weed", three hundred kilometers from home, amid strangers. I wonder how the hell she got there.

On September 11, 2001, someone takes down the Twin Towers in New York, and the western world feels more fragile than ever.

In the village, in addition to grams, rumors start to circulate; it's only few thousand people here, and everyone knows each other. An acquaintance of ours, in fact, is caught by the police with thirteen grams of our weed but tells the agents that he bought it in the city. We realize that we are risking too much, and become more scrupulous, less brazen.

We resolve therefore to draft a kind of regulation in order to avoid troubles of any kind. We only sell to a small group of trusted people, who in turn sell to another couple of trusted contacts and so on. Nothing is to be sold to minors and woe betide if any of our acquaintances do. We avoid travelling too far and invite those who want it to come to us to get it. When we are forced to move, we organize at the same time fake appointments and meetings, to mislead potential checks. I still remember the adrenaline of those days very well. Maybe sometimes we exaggerated with precautions, but doing so ensured that our business went very smoothly.

Nevertheless, the original intentions remain unchanged and, even if we start moving more money, none of us is in it for profit; to the point that one evening, after having smuggled a big batch, we celebrate offering the movie ticket for the countryside cinema, normally desolate. We end up being almost fifty people, a crowd never seen before, watching a random movie.

In all this there is also a positive ethical aspect that I am proud of being able to claim. During that time, thanks to our illicit trafficking of soft drugs we manage to keep away the hard drugs, which rage more and more also in our areas. How? By refusing to sell weed to anyone in contact with those who peddle what we consider "chemical crap". So ecstasy tablets brought by nightclub-goers remain for a while a distance away from the kids of the upper Belluno.

We are young and reckless but aware that "de Marijuana non xe mai morto nisun"[19], while other substances, including those legal and under state monopoly, do serious damage.

But our awareness is as genuine as it is fragile, and is soon jeopardized by the curiosity to go further.

Soon some of our group begins experimenting with other stuff, keeping it hidden from the rest of us.

In the summer of 2002, my parents sent me to London, three months abroad to have a change of scenery, learn to speak English, 'toughen up' and get to know the world. I find work as a kitchen hand in one of the best Italian restaurants in the city, near Green Park.

I work hard and often spend my free time in Camden Town, one of the English capital's most extravagant and colorful suburbs. After a few misfires, the inevitable scam and a couple of extreme raves, I find the right contact to stock up on excellent Orange Bud, high quality cannabis, self-produced in hydroponic culture. The price is very high and I am

---

[19] "No one ever died of Marijuana," verse from a Pitura Freska song, in Venetian dialect.

therefore forced to resell some of it to avoid draining up my finances. The chef of the Michelin-star restaurant I work in becomes my fondest client and as a result, I find out that everybody smokes joints.

And I mean everybody.

In this period I read – or perhaps it is better to say 'I study' – Mr. Nice in the English edition, the autobiography of the international trafficker Howard Marks, released a few months before and still at the top of the sales charts. It seduced me.

On my day off I go to an internet cafe downtown and open my inbox after several weeks offline. There's a new message from a friend of mine, with only two words: "See attachment." It seems like a joke or a virus, but I click on it and it starts to open up a very large image. It slowly loads, from top to bottom. I immediately recognize the header of a well-known local newspaper. It's the first page. The title is now visible and just under I begin to get a glimpse of the great colored photograph in the middle of the cover. I feel the blood drain from my face, and my heartbeat quicken. I look around - fearful that someone may be looking at my screen.

The image has now loaded completely, and the screen shows dozens of cannabis plants, tall and vigorous, uprooted and held by a couple of satisfied and complacent policemen. The article tells of an important anti-drug operation that led to the discovery of a large cultivation of marijuana. They weighed the plants with roots, soil and everything, as often happens in these cases, so the final amount looks enormous. Very. Especially for our region.

The article emphasizes the determination of law enforcement agencies in identifying those responsible. Which thankfully never happens.

Not even the indoor crops that we organized at a friend's house has much more luck. After that blitz, a witch-hunt atmosphere spreads and no one feels like trying their luck anymore.

When I return from London at the end of the summer, everything has changed. Only a few months have passed but they look like years. My group of friends has almost completely fallen apart. Heroin has also arrived and some of us get caught in that cobweb like flies. I write down an emblematic phrase in my diary:

Dynamite-like drugs, explosions of lives.

I distance myself from everyone, including my parents, and isolate myself in a lodge north of Cortina d'Ampezzo where I find a job as a kitchen hand. I spend a confused winter between a thousand joints and bad vibrations. I am beginning to develop an increasingly evident discomfort towards the system. My diary becomes my best friend, the one to whom I address my outburst:

Life is too short to work. Some, many, almost everybody, accepts a life at work. I don't. But I work anyway. Working is stupid, but you have to. Working is losing real time. Some work all their lives because others never work. Those who never work usually have more money than those who work all their life. Money's worth less than shit. For some, many, almost all, money is everything. But it's not their fault. Money is the one to blame.

They are abstract concepts, but ones which I will eventually come across again later on. They will shape my life in a concrete way.

In March 2003 I am almost twenty years old and I write:

Temporarily I am quiet and partly happy, because I like the music I'm listening to and the volume is right; The chocolate joint relaxes me with its well-known effect, and I'm alone, sure that I can't be disturbed. Out there there's a war, in every sense. America, or rather that dickhead Bush, is going to bomb Iraq. Soon, they say, they will strike.

I graduate one year behind schedule and, to celebrate, I go to the Rototom Sunsplash in Osoppo, Udine, one of the largest reggae festivals in Europe. It's like Mecca for us lovers of music, ganja and parties.

I feel particularly predisposed to experimentation and in a short time, I become a psycho-explorer – ignorant and careless. I take acid and spend the next twelve hours in a tiny camping tent, having a bad trip; those hours seemed like a hundred years: I open wide the doors of perception, open the third eye, explore the universe and follow the white rabbit into his hole, risking the ability to turn back. The effect of LSD then vanishes and with it the scariest and greatest adventure of my life. It will take me years to process that experience.

Unhappy, I go back to London with two friends, and we go crazy. Among Mexican mushrooms, incredibly legal in certain Camden Town stores, and Salvia Divinorum, with very high percentages of active compounds, my psychedelic period reaches its peak and at the same time, its end. But it leaves consequences.

I thus understand that the world of hallucinogens is more complex than it seems and should be approached with extreme caution, but above all awareness and knowledge. Features that are not present in a twenty-year-old person, let alone myself.

And it could not be otherwise, since information and awareness are lacking, and talking about it is almost a taboo. Prohibition leads to all this and certainly does not solve the great problems related to abuse and addiction.

The London holiday ends and so does summer: it is time for decisions. In a spurt of enthusiasm, which coincides with a reconciliation between my father and mother, I decide to enroll in university, and I move to Milan to get a Bachelor in Communication at Bergamo.

I have always loved writing, communicating, creating; this is the only walkable path for me.

Chapter 4

THE NEAR MISS REVOLUTION

Hemp history, as we have seen, is quite long, much longer than my personal history with her; but it's at the end of the 18th century that its cultivation in so-called Western countries had an extraordinary development.

In the eighteenth century, in fact, the Industrial Revolution exploded overturning the scheme of things. Not by chance was it called a revolution.

Mechanization broke out in agriculture, and cotton became a popular cultivation: a marginal crop just a few decades before, it now extended halfway around the world, as far as the eye could see.

In natural conditions, cotton could not keep up with Hemp: it had a lower productivity per hectare, needed a lot more water, impoverished the soil, produced less resistant fiber, and was more expensive. But the new discoveries of the time mixed things up: chemical fertilizers and renewed irrigation techniques improved its yield, while the ginning and yarn machines maximized its production, giving the spark to a revolution that was not only agrarian, but also had much deeper political and social ramifications.

During the eighteenth century, European states expanded and strengthened their colonial empires, built centuries earlier, and enlarged their economies by subjugating other populations. Production of raw materials moved where manpower was paid little or nothing, leaving only the processing of the crop to industrial countries. And where the local work force wasn't large enough, new laborer were smuggled in with violence. The new cotton industry was in fact highly dependent on slavery.

England and France produced their own fabric needs at low prices in the Caribbean colonies where in just seven years – between 1784 and 1790 – two hundred and fifty thousand African slaves were imported. The United States adopted a different strategy: not having colonies (as they were a colony themselves), they enslaved their own people solely on the basis of race. Starting in Georgia and South Carolina, and then in Alabama, Louisiana, Mississippi, Arkansas and Texas. In a few years over a million men reduced to chains docked in the United States, forced to sweat in plantations in exchange for a piece of bread, while the extermination of native peoples intensified with pondered brutality[20]: land had to be cleared in order to make room for plantations, at any cost.

The harvested cotton travelled through the railways to the new cities of the West, where masses of wage-earners – men only apparently freer than African deportees – deteriorated among the toxic fumes of fabric factories. For those collecting the profits everything worked a treat: production increased, and costs kept on dropping. In 1776 a cotton shirt cost up to two hundred times more than a comparable Hemp product - a century later it cost half[21].

At the beginning of the twentieth century paper was subjected to a similar process. Hemp paper was almost indestructible, but it was also rather laborious to produce. The separation of hurd and bast fiber was still done by hand: it needed time and men. But the new publishing industry wanted to save on both and didn't care much about quality. The new rewarding game was in fact selling newspapers: millions of copies distributed every day, whose sheets had to be thin and didn't have to last more than twenty-four hours. There was a raw material perfectly suited for the purpose, particularly because it came from one of the more abundant and cheap sources present in nature: forests.

At the beginning of the century therefore, a machine capable of chopping the trunks of trees in a few minutes was invented; the shredded material was then treated with sodium bisulfite and oil to get a paste to

---

[20] The nineteenth century is the one in which the so-called "final solution" against native peoples was implemented. The generals were given carte blanche, massacres and reprisals against the tribes intensified, concentration camps (the "Indian reserves") were planned and built and laws such as the Indian Removal Act were passed. An Act that, in 1830, authorized the deportation of natives for unspecified "national security reasons". In the Americas, both north and south, between 1492 and 1890, between 70 and 115 million native people were exterminated.

[21] Herer J., *The Emperor wears no clothes*, Op. Cit.

laid out in sheets and then left to dry. The color was not great, but with an abundant use of another chemical solvent – chlorine – it became perfectly white.

Publishing had its new paper indeed, available in abundance and at an unbeatable price. Forests were not thankful, nor were the lungs of paper mill workers, but they were minor details for those who pulled the strings of the economy.

Throughout this triumph of "progress", Hemp did not disappear altogether as her fiber remained essential in the manufacturing of ropes, nets and paper and fabrics of higher quality, but she certainly lost some relevance. She simply wasn't competitive anymore because she had not hooked up on to the train of the Industrial Revolution. Her proverbial resistance had become a defect. Ginning machines, that had made the fortune of cotton, were not robust enough to process Hemp, while the tools capable of crushing entire trunks of a tree in a matter of seconds couldn't overcome the elasticity of her stems. So, the plant was still processed in a traditional way.

The trunks were collected in sheafs, then left to steep for at least a week to dissolve the gelatinous substance (pectin) between the fibers and skin (a process called retting). Once dry, the stalks went through the "breaking" process, using a specific wooden lever tool, which was long, bulky and difficult to maneuver, and often required specialized labor. Only after this further step was the tow obtained, that is Hemp fiber, which had to be cleaned and beaten to eliminate residual impurities before being able to be processed.

Where industrialization was still in its infant stage – as in Russia and Italy – Hemp was still the most used harvest for textile purposes[22], but in the part of the world that was rushing towards a society of mass consumption, her processing was too slow and complicated to keep up.

---

[22] In 1940, in Italy, ninety thousand hectares of land were employed for the cultivation of Hemp, which is a surface larger than the one occupied globally in 2011 for such crop.

However, cannabis was too valuable to remain long forgotten in the annals of history: it only took a few more decades to discover the right technical solutions to bring her into modernity.

In 1917 in fact, George Schlichten, a German who migrated to the US, patented the decorticator. It was a specially modified reaper-binder[23]: it was enough to insert Hemp into the gearwheel, where an automatic chain conveyor took her to a rotating arm capable of breaking the plant, separating the fiber from the stalk. The latter was shredded and fell into the tremor, then a compressor blew the stalks towards the packaging machine, from where they emerged already wrapped up. The fibers instead were sent to the binder, that returned them divided into neat bundles, ready for processing.

It was during the years of World War I and it took a while to find the funding necessary for the realization of prototypes, but the invention immediately attracted great attention. The patent was still being released when the United States Department of Agriculture, in its official bulletin, spoke of a machine that once developed will bring back Hemp to be the major national agricultural industry[24].

Schlichten's invention was revived in the 1930s, when studies on the use of Hemp fiber increased. New studies focused also on the production of plastic and cellulose. A new technique to get paper directly from pulp and no longer from fiber was designed. Until then, in fact, pulp had been considered a by-product of processing, despite making up more than 70% of the stalk. The first decorticators were put into operation in Texas, Minnesota and Illinois, where they proved that they could guarantee speedy production at competitive prices compared to those of cotton for fabrics and trees for paper.

Hemp was preparing to reclaim her historical role, that of the essential plant for humanity. And I'm not exaggerating. It's enough to have a look at the press release of that time of two important trade magazines. On 26 February 1937, an article titled The most profitable &

---

[23] The reaper-binder was a machine for harvesting and tying grains like wheat and oats, and later outdated by the most modern combine harvester

[24] *USDA Bulletin* 404, 1916.

desirable crop that can be grown appeared in Mechanical Engineering, stressing for the first time the sustainable qualities of the plant:

> Hemp, the strongest of the vegetable fibers, gives the greatest production per acre and requires the least attention. [...] Recent floods and dust storms have given warnings against the destruction of timber. Possibly, the hitherto waste products of flax and Hemp may yet meet a good part of that need, especially in the plastics field which is growing by leaps and bounds[25].

The following year the magazine Popular Mechanics published an article that listed all possible applications of cannabis in manufacturing. It's striking to read it today, starting from the title: New billion-dollar crop. It stated how the plant could be used to produce:

> ... more than 5,000 textile products, ranging from rope to fine laces [...] more than 25,000 products, ranging from dynamite to Cellophane [...] Hemp will produce every grade of paper, and government figures estimate that 10,000 acres devoted to Hemp will produce as much paper as 40,000 acres[26] of average pulp land[27].

Sounds contemporary, doesn't it?

Yet, while writing this article, the magazine editors were not aware of the studies that the largest American automobile factory – Ford – had been conducting in secret since 1929. Cars were about to become a mass product and required large amounts of metal, plastic and oil. Henry Ford, though, was deeply convinced that the car of the future should be built and fueled with biodegradable components. His engineers were working on a car entirely built with natural fibers taken from flax, Hemp and straw

---

[25] *The most profitable & desirable crop that can be grown*, Mechanical Engineering Magazine, n. 2, 1937.

[26] An American acre corresponds to 0.404686 hectares, or 4046,873 meters Square.

[27] *New billion-dollar crop*, in Popular Mechanics Magazine, n. 2, 1938.

and entirely fueled by Hemp ethanol[28]. A few more months and the prototype would have been presented to the world.

Paper, plastic, cars, fuel. Once again, she could have revolutionized everything.

She could have. But while humanity was caught between two terrible world conflicts, a new war never told in history books had already begun. And Hemp was the target.

---

[28] Rowan Robinson, *The Great Book of Hemp*, Bear & Co., 1996.

Chapter 5

GHOSTS AND THE COMMUNITY

In September 2003 my main focus is Milan: I want to start university and turn the page.

I move to the city, coming from a small mountain village, and I discover a concrete jungle. I feel cosmopolitan and at the same time restless and thrilled by this new lifestyle.

I attend Communication lessons the beautiful Bergamo Alta Campus, together with hundreds of other fresh and jaunty students, proud of their high school graduations.

I immediately feel like an odd duck, but I try to resist and get infected by collective enthusiasm. I'm not alone, Luca is with me, a friend from Belluno with whom I share mainly two passions: music and joints. But there is no longer the light-heartedness of previous years. Everything has changed and the weight of responsibilities and the pressure to progress begins to be felt more and more.

University is much less engaging than I imagined. The classrooms are overcrowded, the professors read out their lessons like robots, without any enthusiasm or pathos, the topics are boring and as useless as in high school, outdated textbooks are taken as gospel. No one ever dares to question anything, everybody with their heads down writing notes without ever going outside the margins of the notebooks. I'm disappointed, I expected more.

Meanwhile in the canton of Ticino, a few kilometers from Milan, Hemp shops manage to sell weed thanks to a decoy, as environmental perfumers: a quibble in the law allows them to legally sell ganja of extraordinary quality; among the most popular varieties, *Super Pink Skunk, Northern Light and Diam*. We get there a few weeks late, when the government is aware of the phenomenon – and of the revolving doors of thousands of Milanese who go to stock up every weekend – and takes action by changing the law and closing all the "diffusers". We still find the same offer in the parks of Chiasso, and we stock up as former growers, now jobless and as improvised pushers. It's very strong marijuana, with high THC content. It only takes a few tokes to get high. Too high at times. With this comes the first paranoia and the first "ghosts".

One day, after a pot bong and a weed joint combo, I end up literally lying-in bed, curled up like freezing and confused child, as has never happened before. It's an effect that I don't like, it upsets and agitates me, the exact opposite of what was happening in the past. I decide to stop and, after years of smoking almost on a daily basis, I interrupt one of my favorite habits, starting a long period of abstinence. Among my notes I write:

> *I'm living strange days, often sad days. But this is nothing new. I can't shake off the agitation. I know that time will fix everything,, but it's not easy waiting for sunny days, knowing that my sunny days should be these ones. Demons. Shadows. Bad vibes. Darkness. Inside me, Guernica. But I dream at night and in the morning I remember well what I dreamed about, which hadn't happened to me in a long time. I quit smoking and that makes me lucid, responsive, with my feet closer to the ground. I feel that it's important to me, I feel like I've made the right choice, for my present and above all for my future.*

Ghosts – in spite of myself – remain to keep me company from time to time, university proceeds slowly and I throw myself headlong into a new project.

With Luca I decide to open a website that talks about cannabis and related topics. We want to create a virtual place where you can find news and information about the anti-prohibitionist and psychedelic culture that are normally difficult to find. We want also to talk about special journeys and underground movements who often struggle to find space in traditional media.

None of us are webmasters or programmers and we have zero funds available. I study the basics of HTML coding and with my self-taught skills I publish the first sloppy version of *Enjoint*, "the first Italian community dedicated to peace, love and legalization".

Ghosts and the community

In December 2003, Saddam Hussein is captured. I read Robinson Crusoe by Daniel Defoe and it changes my life. I write down two passages of the book that still today – fifteen years later – represent the foundations of my existence more and more:

> *All our discontents about what we want, appear to me to spring from the want of thankfulness for what we have.*

What a great truth! So obvious yet so difficult to put in practice. And even more valuable:

> I learned to look more upon the bright side of my condition, and less upon the dark side, and to consider what I enjoyed rather than what I wanted.

Enjoint occupies most of my days. I soon realize the infinite developments that it can have and what it can offer thanks to internet. There is a lot of interest, with users asking for content, and others reach out wanting to cooperate. We open a discussion forum on a free platform and the community begins to take shape. We virtually meet people scattered throughout Italy who have the same interests. It doesn't feel real.

I write in the diary:

> *My serenity is still far away, but I am sure I am on the right path.. I often have sudden mood swings, but the ghosts are leaving me, slowly. I often feel lost, empty, and deep in my past, in those days and moments of fear and delirium.*

In February 2004, Marco Pantani dies. I'm starting to mature the idea that mass media rarely tells us the truth, and my desire to create an alternative voice in the information landscape grows day-by-day. I follow with interest the university class on theories and techniques in media language, where a good professor shows us how newspapers are able to exploit any news according to their needs and directives imposed from above. I learn that the few spared from this are local newspapers, but only because they have more humble ambitions. National newspapers are, for the most part, scrap paper. I study the subject and give my first and only university exam; I score 29/30, one of the highest marks of the class.

I have a chat with the professor and communicate to him my intention to drop out of university. He replies that I'd be a fool after such a good first exam, but he partly understands my choice. I take some time to think and continue attending some other classes. During a crowded Editorial Marketing lesson, the lecturer comes out with this gem: "There are two hundred of you here, but only one of you – perhaps – will become a journalist; everyone else will end up working in some press office doing photocopies or meaningless tasks."

At that precise moment I get up, leave the classroom, and decide that that one journalist would be me.

In the spring I sign the first advertising contract for *Enjoint* with a company in Genoa that buys a yearly banner for five hundred Euros. It's just over forty Euro a month, but I already feel like I'm Bill Gates. I reinvest it all on the website to develop it further.

Thanks to two other sponsors we print the first flyers for our community; they read:

> *We are looking for people tired of being silent, fresh minds with something to say, people who know how to have fun while gathering ideas, projects, initiatives, thoughts and words on the true world of young people, made up of parties, journeys and hopes. Everyone will be able to read, everyone will be able to write.*

And on the back:

> *Enjoint, Italy's first community for peace, love and legalization. Over 650 registered users in 5 months. Enjoint is a non-profit, independent project, free from any political link. It aims to give space to the new generation's thoughts, trying, at the same time, to keep contact with all the realities that already exist and operate in the industry. It is against prohibition, wars, violence and narcotraffickers.*

I quit university and my parents – justly – cut off my financial support. I'm forced to look for a job to make a living, so I pass from a copy shop to a company of floral decorations, but as soon as I get back at home, I throw myself on the computer to improve *Enjoint*. I love to dedicate myself to what interests me, to give life to my creativity and passion. I give all of myself to what I believe in.

And soon a few doors open up. In June 2004, I receive an important call. A well-known Dutch magazine dedicated to cannabis, already present in various European countries, wants to publish in Italy. It is a bimonthly free publication. Given the good work done with *Enjoint* up to that point, they want me to be their editor. They're not only asking me to run a newsroom, they're asking me to create it from scratch, in a few months. They want to test me and they give me their trust. For me it's a dream, the opportunity I was looking for. I give my heart and soul to this project, sleeping few hours per night and spending my days in front of the PC, between phone calls and emails, sometimes even skipping meals.

In the summer I meet Franco Casalone, considered one of the gurus of Hemp in Italy, author of historical books such as *Hemp shops and indoor culture*. It's an important meeting for me, beyond the professional connection. Surprisingly, it gives me some precious reading keys to understanding the experiences I've had in the past with drugs that still upset me. I don't think I ever thanked him enough, so I want to take the chance in this book to do it. Finally, I convince him to write for the magazine that's about to be born, and he's an important figure in the list of collaborators.

In August, Dr. Fabrizio Cinquini – surgeon who has often incriminated himself regarding his own cannabis plantations, cultivated in order to donate them to patients with serious pathologies such as multiple sclerosis and cancer – invites me to Versilia to tell me about his studies and anti-prohibitionist projects. I take the train and get to Viareggio station in the late afternoon, where he's waiting for me in his car. We travel a few dozen kilometers inland, through the hills, and we finally get to his house, surrounded by the greenery of the countryside. It is almost dusk, and the visibility is not great. Cinquini invites me to stay for the night in a nice room on the second floor. It is not yet clear to me what I'm doing here and above all what the doctor wants to show me. The next morning someone wakes me up yelling my name from the courtyard:

«Matteo! Matteo! »

I get up and open my shutters. It's Dr. Cinquini who greets me a good morning with his irrepressible energy and joy of life. With my eyes still half-closed, I try to focus on the view. I rub my eyes and raise my eyebrows in surprise: in front of me is an almost endless stretch of huge cannabis plants, starting a few steps from the house and extending over the adjacent hills. It's clear to me from the very first moment that this is not industrial Hemp. Those plants obviously bleed THC. Cinquini opens his arms towards them as a conductor, ecstatic, and he loudly exclaims:

"Matteo, look at this beauty!".

I smile looking at him and at the biggest outdoor cultivation I've ever seen it in my life. But the smile fades quickly away, as soon as I realize that, in the event of a police raid, I would probably end up in jail with no ifs or buts.

But Fabrizio quickly regains my attention by saying:

"Matteo, please go to the kitchen and pull the curtain to the left of the fridge. Take one of those bags and throw it to me."

"What should I throw at you, Fabrizio?"

"A bag, a bag, don't worry, go and get one."

I follow the instructions and go in the kitchen of the apartment and see the long, colored curtain. I slide it to the side and I'm standing in front of four large wooden shelves carrying dozens of bags of marijuana inflorescence, ready to use. I take one and go back to the window. Fabrizio is still out there and he extends his hands towards me:

«Throw it, throw it! »

I throw the half a kilo of flowers at him in a surreal scene, afraid to find myself victim of a candid camera.

"Come on, Matteo, come down for breakfast. Then I'll take you for a tour in the fields and show you my watch-ostriches."

Ghosts and the community

It's all true, and this is the incredible world of Dr. Fabrizio Cinquini, a pioneer, a visionary, who will soon give life to Cannabis Strong Type, the first Hemp trade expo in Italy, in Pescia in the province of Pistoia.

At the end of summer, meeting the deadline I was given, I close and deliver the first issue of the magazine. The Dutch share their satisfaction with a blunt "Excellent job, Mr. Gracis".

Unlike the other European editions, where translated archive items are traditionally used, the Italian one already presents, in its first issue, more than 70% new content. I not only deliver a complete magazine, but also a staff of competent and carefully selected editors, plus new editorial features that will continue for many years to come.

I am becoming more and more dedicated to the editorial work, while I'm still publishing *Enjoint*.

I write down in my loyal diary:

> Today Milan was beautiful! The sun shined upon it, the square in the CBD was full of people. A black boy sitting on the steps of the Duomo sang loudly. Colors and sounds, scents. Yep, today Milan was beautiful. I went shopping. And then, walking towards St. Babila in the midst of all those people, I asked myself if I too, inexorably, was surrendering to that consumerism that sucks the lifeblood to our souls. I got no answer yet, but I think that pondering this over time will do me some good.. Sometimes I feel like a living contradiction, at time victim and at time complicit, a little cowardly perhaps. After all, wouldn't life be easier without thinking about these things?

On 26 December 2004, a fierce tsunami causes three hundred thousand deaths in Southeast Asia. I am astonished at the images coming from Indonesia and Thailand, countries I came to know years earlier while traveling with my parents. I do what I can to create a web initiative to raise money and provide the latest information. I also involve *Enjoint* and the whole community.

And I print a quote from the Dalai Lama to hang right above my computer to have it always in front of my eyes: "Let us try to recognize the precious nature of each day". I still look upon this mantra to this day, and try to honor it throughout my life.

At the end of January 2005, I participate in the *Highlife* trade show in Utrecht, Netherlands, invited by my editors. Here for the first time, I come into real contact with what is now known as "cannabusiness", i.e. the business that revolves around the world of cannabis, legal or not.

Since the late 1960s, with the rise of hippy culture, the use of Hemp for recreational purposes has spread exponentially, despite fierce prohibition. In that period the first growers entered the scene, consumers who, in order to avoid relying on narcotraffic, cultivated the plant themselves, all out in the open, but always away from prying eyes, being still an illegal practice and prosecutable. It was still an experimental phase – a discrete but concrete action of civil disobedience. Since the mid-1990s indoor cultivation has developed in various European countries. Unlike that of the outdoors, it has two great advantages: it allows you to control temperature, light, any possible insect infestations and avoid negative atmospheric outcomes; but above all it exposes the grower to much less risk. With a few square meters in your basement used as a grow room[29] it is easy to manage and almost impossible to discover. The trade tools are vases, soil, special lamps, air purifiers and conditioners, purification and extraction equipment, cabinets or boxes for cultivation, known as grow boxes, fertilizers and above all, seeds.

Cannabis seeds are legal almost everywhere, since they do not contain an active substance and are therefore not considered a drug, though they are sold for collecting or for the preservation of varieties, by law they cannot be grown. Yes, you heard right: you can buy seeds and everything you need to cultivate them, but as you put them in the earth you become a bandit.

The real paradox, however, is not this one, but the fact that we made outlawed a plant that grows spontaneously in nature.

The fact remains that around this practice of production, a flourishing market – literally – was created, with grow shops in its epicenter, that is stores that specialize in cultivation tools and necessities. Over time they

---

[29] Space entirely designated for the cultivation.

have evolved and opened up to other products linked to the world of Hemp, such as food, textiles, cosmetics and consumer items such as bongs, Chillums and vaporizers. A niche but booming market, which finds its best showcase right specialized expos, like the one in Utrecht where I stood.

The exhibition is very well structured and professional. After all, Holland, at the moment, is the center of the "cannabis world", thanks to its tolerant laws allowing the purchase and consumption of marijuana in coffee-shops. To me it is a totally new world and I study it with dedication to understand its dynamics and succeed in doing well at my job. The editors of the magazine look after me and introduced me to sponsors and companies as the 'Italian wunderkind'.

I write on my agenda:

> *I am glad to have returned to life after a long period of shadows and ghosts. They still keep me company at times, but nothing compared to before. And especially now I know how to recognize and manage them.*

I am twenty-two years old and that spring I get to know Michele "Haze Man", a countryman almost my own age but already among the highest experts of cannabis varieties. A true "joint-sommelier". I remain enchanted by his talent in smelling weed tips and recognizing the strain.

We soon become friends and this connection inspires important ideas for future initiatives, first of all *Magical Italy*, a yearly publication taking a full census of over one hundred and twenty grow shops present in Italy.

This is my first commercial project in the industry, since *Enjoint* was and will always be non-profit. I'm excited and the first people I speak to about it are the Dutch publishers, both for fairness and for exploring a possible collaboration between the magazine and my coming guide. Oddly, my communication is followed by a few days of total silence. I don't get a response for a while, until an email of few lines arrives, in which they communicate to me with a disarming detachment that my working relationship with them is over. I go through the email many times, incredulous. Maybe I mistranslated. It's not possible.

The decision is not justified in any way nor are there any complaints. Moreover, three numbers of the bimonthly magazine have come out and at each publication has performed better than the last. Everything was on a roll.

And yet they just fired me.

I ask for explanations and after a few emails following up, finally get a reply: they believe that I am becoming too entrepreneurial and those who work for them cannot have personal projects in the industry. They too have a guide of Dutch grow shops and will soon expand it by featuring Italian's ones: they see mine as a possible inconvenient competitor. I offer to give up the idea of Magical Italy, because the magazine is undoubtedly my priority, but the answer is always 'no' and their decision is final.

After all the staff is now set up, their free press is well-established even in Italy, therefore my presence is no longer crucial or necessary. They replace me easily. I stumbled upon the cynicism and cowardice of yellow-bellied businessman.

It's a shock. I put my soul into that job and now feel betrayed. But there is no room for despair and I react.

I write down:

Balance, in victories and defeats. Matteo, go your own way.

What right there seemed to me to be an extremely negative episode in my life, would prove to be a fundamental turning point. I have to acknowledge that every cloud has a silver lining.

I quickly set aside the matter and stay focused on my projects. I decide that I want to know more about the subject and that I should know it in detail if I want to make a job out of it. I delve into readings, documentaries and research the history of Hemp, and I learn about a universe that I totally ignored. I discover the incredible variety of uses of this plant, the role that she played in our past, but above all I learn how in the last century someone managed to banish it, deceiving the whole world.

Ghosts and the community

Hemp, an incredible story

Chapter 6

WITCH HUNT

Cannabis – as we have seen – has been a fundamental plant to human development for millennia, but in the 1930s, just as she was preparing to become again "the most fruitful and attractive crop" it was prohibited. And the prohibition did not fall only on what the newspapers of the time renamed marijuana, but they carefully devised a way to ban the use of every part of the plant, for every possible purpose.

Who took such an absurd and apparently self-harming decision? And most importantly, why?

To line up the dots of this story, you may get the impression that you're reading a carefully planned thriller. Those thrillers in which the interests of the villains have mysterious ties who, thanks to the support of journalists and crooked politicians, succeed in legitimizing their plan, managing not only to make it possible, but even appealing in the eyes of the viewer.

And so, to understand how it unfolded, all that remains is to start from the beginning.

The first protagonist of this story is William Randolph Hearst: US publishing magnate, Hearst owned gossip magazines and dozens of local newspapers around major cities. His fortune was thanks to the rise of what Americans called "yellow journalism", scandalous journalism made of squealing headings, news magnified or invented out of thin air. In other words, Hearst is the progenitor of tabloids and fake news that surround us still. He sold hundreds of thousands of copies per day and, working in the industry, had sensed another fruitful affair: cultivating trees for paper production. For this purpose, he had purchased land throughout California, his state of residence, and in neighboring Mexico, becoming in a few years the leading cellulose manufacturer in all the United States. The industry was so profitable that it allowed Hearst to live in a castle of fifty-eight bedrooms and a swimming pool designed on the model of the temples of ancient Rome.

Hemp, an incredible story

The second protagonist is Lammot Du Pont, who in those same years, with his brother Pierre, was taking the family business through a product conversion: from explosives and gunpowder production to materials sciences and polymers vital to modern manufacturing. Since the 1920s he registered patents for petroleum-derived materials that would become famous across the world, such as Nylon, Naflon, Lycra and Teflon. With these compounds, in fact, he started the manufacture of multiple objects that would soon be of common use (stockings, underwear, dresses, umbrellas, sheets, brushes, ropes, packaging and much more) and he was about to become a world leader in petrochemistry.

Hearst and Du Pont were united by the fact that their respective investment fields were put at serious risk by the progress made by the Hemp industry.

And this is where the third protagonist of our story comes into play, namely Andrew Mellon, one of the leading bankers of the time, who had precisely financed Hearst and Du Pont. Mellon was not only a banker though: he was also the U.S. Secretary of Treasury and above all he was the owner of *Gulf Oil*, one of the oil industry's famous "seven sisters". He too saw that the expansion of his industry was directly threatened by cannabis because, as shown by the experiments conducted by Henry Ford, the plant was indeed an effective, clean and economic fuel.

Finally, the fourth protagonist, John Rockefeller, another great banker, as well as owner of *Standard Oil*, a company that was invading the United States with its own gas stations. Rockefeller was among the main financiers of the pharmaceutical industries, the same ones that in future would be known as big pharma, which in those years were focused on fine-tuning synthetic medicines with the aim of abandoning less profitable drugs of natural origin, i.e. products made by any kind of plants or herb - cannabis above all.

We are therefore faced with a natural alliance between the paper, chemical, oil and pharmaceutical industries, all determined to use their economic and political power to get that horrific plant out of their way, the one that, with her thousand uses, risked turning them all belly up.

This is the hypothesis formulated by some scholars and journalists of international reputation, starting with Jack Herer, author of "The

Emperor wears no clothes", the book that first highlighted the plot of relationships and interests that connects the protagonists just described.

The conspiracy theory against Hemp however is not universally accepted and other following studies have attempted to minimize Herer's claims, accusing him of having published his own theory without sufficient evidence. The fact that almost a century has passed did the rest: no protagonist or direct witness can be heard from anymore, and it's unlikely that we'll ever be able to shed further light on what happened behind the scenes of this staging.

Fortunately for us, there are many facts that we can list in search of the objective truth.

In the early years of the last century, the United States became a land of massive immigration from Mexico, thanks in large part to the civil war that erupted after the uprising of revolutionaries led by Emiliano Zapata and Francisco Pancho Villa. In 1929, with the great depression, many Americans lost their jobs, exacerbating existing racial tensions. The many Mexicans then became a problem, accused of not integrating into society and by providing cheap labor, stealing jobs from Americans. The same old story of the scapegoat, in short.

Many Mexican workers smoked cannabis in the evening to relax, in the same way that Americans drank whisky. The use of Hemp was so common among immigrants that in the original version of the famous Mexican folk song *La Cucaracha* the revolutionaries, in the refrain, are looking for "marijuana to smoke"[30].

William Hearst, with his newspapers rode the wave, ready to strike two birds with one stone. After all, the publishing magnate is portrayed by his biographers as a staunch racist, especially towards Mexicans, after the revolutionaries led by Pancho Villa occupied almost a million hectares of his paper tree-growing land in northern Mexico.

---

[30] In the original version a verse says: "*The cockroach, the cockroach, can no longer walk; because it doesn't have, because it lacks marijuana to smoke*». In the version that became famous around the world decades later the expression "*marijuana to smoke*" was replaced by "*Money to spend*".

Hemp, an incredible story

After all, in those days in the United States, not many people were looking for marijuana to smoke recreationally No one even knew what the word marijuana meant. The Americans called it cannabis or Hemp and they knew this plant for its multiple industrial and medical uses, preserving at home extracts or packets of cigarettes already rolled as a remedy for numerous malaises. A crusade against cannabis would have not made sense to their eyes.

That's why Hearst decided to use the plant's Mexican nickname for his battle. A difference that appeared to be lexical, but served to muddy the waters and help hide his own political goal: describing Hemp as a diabolical plant would not have been accepted by the population, but doing the same using the mysterious nickname marijuana, and hence associating it with the growing distrust towards ethnic minorities, could work. And it did.

Words alone cannot describe the work that the Hearst newspapers did to instill in Americans the terror of this strange drug. One only has to read any of those articles, published in their hundreds in those years, to get a sense.

They make Marijuana into cigarettes nowadays, didn't you know that? Oh, yes, plenty of Marijuana cigarettes on the market, they call them "Silly Smokes," when they sell them. Marijuana is really hashish, an American hashish. In India and in the Malay Peninsula they call hashish the murder drug, and we are beginning to hear American hashish, marijuana, called murder smoke here in police circles. The police know all about murder smoke. Whenever a particularly cruel and revolting crime is committed and the criminal gets away, the police start hunting for the murder smoke users. That baby that was found in a woodshed the other day tortured almost beyond human belief? Who tortured that poor helpless infant? Nobody knows, yet they are looking for someone who smokes "murder smoke."

Those women, three different ones in three different parts of the country, who were saturated with gasoline and set on fire, are these "Murder Smoke" murders? Ten chances to one they were. How about the two young men

> who tortured a poor girl in the stone quarry near San Francisco the other night, disfigured her for life--a good girl with a good reputation--were these two young fiends "Murder Smokers"? Ask the police, they'll tell you a tale about "Murder Smoke" crimes, a tale that will freeze the warmest blood in the calmest veins.
>
> Marijuana is sometimes brewed into a tea, sometimes it is snuffed -from the crown of the thumb like cocaine, but more often these days it is rolled into a cigarette. The first "Murder Smoke" cigarette, brings, strange and weirdly beautiful dreams, but after the first few cigarettes it takes more and more smoking to produce the dream, and suddenly the tortured nerves give way and the "Murder Smoker' must cut and stab, and beat and shoot, to satisfy the tortured hunger created by the drug. "Silly Smoke"-- how much do you know about it? And how do you know when it will to turn into "Murder Smoke"?[31]

I know, it seems impossible. But these quoted words filled the heads of millions of Americans.

The follies about murder smoke, obsessively repeated on all Hearst's newspapers, served to frighten the white petite bourgeoisie, great consumers of tabloids and swing voters in elections where the right was still denied to Blacks and to most Hispanics. The effect was impressive. Marijuana was demonized for targeting ethnic minorities, and minorities demonized to hit Hemp. A perverse vortex that became unstoppable in a few months, generating a social alarm that led the Los Angeles Police Chief to say that marijuana was "the most dangerous drug of all, " and that countless crimes were committed because of its effect; while his counterpart in New Orleans went even further, stating that "reefer makes darkies think they're as good as white men"[32]. Arguments that were

---

[31] *Mother sacrifices children, home, reputation for dope*, in The San Francisco Examiner, 27 February 1930.

[32] J. Helmer, *Drugs and minority oppression*, Seabury Press, 1975.

reminiscent of the race fanaticism of Hitler and Mussolini[33] were becoming more and more frequent in the parlance of white Americans, reiterated even from scientific journals, such as the Medical and Surgical Journal which in 1931 wrote:

> *The dominant race and most enlightened countries are alcoholic, whilst the races and nations addicted to Hemp and opium [...] have deteriorated both mentally and physically [...] The possible substitution of alcohol for a greater evil should be considered the greatest possible calamity that can befall a nation*[34].

The gossip and conservative press – both Hearst's and others – kept adding irons to the fire, repeating itself over and over. A hodgepodge that didn't spare even the Black music par-excellence. Blacks and Mexicans were painted as crazy beasts who, under the effect of the terrible murder smoke, played their "satanic voodoo music" united against whites and against the social order. The music Hearst's lackeys were talking about was jazz, described as "the result of wild and uncontrollable visions caused by marijuana consumption"[35].

But more was needed to translate these fears into legal measures. It was necessary to attribute this set of delirious theories with scientific truth based on evidence. And it wasn't easy, not least because some research on the effects of marijuana had already been carried out, giving the opposite results desired by its enemies.

At the end of the nineteenth century, the British Empire commissioned research within the Indian colony with the specific objective of verifying the possible negative effects of cannabis, widely used in that society. Over three thousand pages of reports on the study of 1200 consumers stated:

---

[33] In the 1930s Mussolini declared that Cannabis was "*enemy of the race*" and "*drug of the nigger*", thus beginning a criminalization of its use, at the time not very widespread in Italy.

[34] A.E. Fossier, *The Marihuana Menace*, in Medical and Surgical Journal, ottobre1931.

[35] J. Herer, M. Brockers, *Canapa, cannabis, marijuana*, Cotton Words Editions,1991.

> *Opinion is [...] of the moderate use being harmless. [...] excessive use may certainly be accepted as very injurious, though it must be admitted that in many excessive consumers injury is not clearly marked. The injury done by excessive use is, however, confined almost exclusively to the consumer himself; the effect on society is rarely appreciable*[36].

Similarly, research commissioned by the United States Army on the effects of cannabis among soldiers in the Panama Canal, among which consumption had spread to barracks, stated without hesitation that:

> *There is no evidence that marijuana as grown here is a "habit-forming" drug in the sense in which the term is applied to alcohol, opium, cocaine, etc., or that it has any appreciably deleterious influence on the individuals using it*[37].

The report, prepared by a group of psychiatrists who had observed for weeks the cannabis-using soldiers, ended with a recommendation:

> *"No steps be taken by the Canal Zone authorities to prevent the sale or use of marijuana, and that no special legislation be asked for."*

So, anything but murder smoke! According to the only American scientific research available at the time, the only effects produced by marijuana on the psyche were "laughing without proper cause and sometimes talking foolishly."

At the beginning of the 1930s the prohibition of alcohol was now at its conclusion as, since it was introduced in 1919, it had only produced huge profits for the mafia, and health damage for wider society due to the placing on the market of poisoned substances. Yet, in 1931 the aforementioned banker Andrew Mellon, as Secretary of the Treasury, appointed Harry J. Anslinger, his niece's husband, Commissioner of the Federal Bureau of Narcotics. Anslinger, an ambitious bureaucrat of

---

[36] *Indian Hemp Drug Commission, Report 1893-1894*, Vol. 1.

[37] J.F. Siler et al., *Marijuana Smoking in Panama*, in The Military Surgeon, vol. 73,1933.

puritanical ideas, spent years as Inspector at the Bureau of Prohibition, the office that was supposed to counter – in truth with little success – the spread of alcohol smuggling. Anslinger was precisely the political connection needed by Hearst for his battle against cannabis. In a few months the anti-alcohol propaganda ceased, but the same arguments were used instead to invoke the prohibition of the new "demon", providing "scientific" coverage to the sensationalist and racist shots of the newspapers.

Anslinger commenced intense activity, writing articles, speaking on radio, organizing conferences, all with a single goal: to convince the public, and politicians, of the need to take action against Cannabis, tying its consumption to unlawfulness in practically every piece of crime news.

A summary of the content of his campaign against cannabis is well expressed in this statement:

> *"The drug (Marijuana) is adhering to its old-world traditions of murder, assault, rape, physical demoralization and mental breakdown. [...] Bureau records prove that its use is associated with insanity and crime. Therefore, from the standpoint of police work, it is a more dangerous drug than heroin or cocaine*[38]*."*

The battle was reaching its climax.

In 1936, a Puritan Catholic group with US$100,000, financed the production of a movie against marijuana titled "Tell Your Children". Sixty-eight minutes of film that did nothing but show young people who, after smoking a joint, abandoned themselves to the most heinous crimes and gestures, such as throwing themselves out of the window in prey to hysterical laughter.

The following year came "Assassin of youth" – practically a clone of the previous movie – whose script was built on written work of the same name published by Anslinger himself and financed by the US Government.

---

[38] *Local "Reliefer" Held for Selling Marihuana*, in Janesville Daily Gazette, 9February 1938.

Public opinion was now properly indoctrinated. Millions of Americans now believed that masses of immigrants, turned crazy by the terrible murder drug, roamed the streets in search of blood, and none of the public understood that marijuana was nothing more than cannabis, the same substance they regularly kept in the medicine drawer[39].

Anslinger then went on targeting the US Senate: he wanted to convince the government to pass a law to ban cannabis at the Federal level. Firstly, he provided what he renamed the *Gore File*, which was the collection of two hundred cases of various crimes which, in his opinion, were all induced by Marijuana consumption. Then he went directly to the US Congress, invited to illustrate his studies on cannabis. In front of American elected representatives, he declared:

> "About 50% of all violent crimes committed in the U.S. were committed by Spaniards, Mexican-Americans, Latin Americans, Filipinos, African-Americans and Greeks, and these crimes could be traced directly to marijuana.
> [...] There are 100,000 total marijuana smokers in the U.S., and most are Negroes, Hispanics, Filipinos and entertainers. Their Satanic music, jazz and swing result from marijuana use. This marijuana causes white women to seek sexual relations with Negroes, entertainers and any others.[40]"

Anslinger's goal was to get a law banning altogether the Hemp plant and all its components, including seeds[41]. So in the summer of 1936, when he was appointed to represent the United States during the debate on the *Convention for the Suppression of the Illicit Traffic in Dangerous*

---

[39] As of 1937, there were at least twenty-eight medicinal products containing Cannabis regularly for sale in U.S. pharmacies.

[40] R.J. Gerber, *Legalizing Marijuana: Drug Policy Reform and Prohibition Politics,* Greenwood Press, 2004.

[41] At the end of 1936, in the wake of anti-marijuana press campaigns, forty-six of forty-eight American States had already passed laws in which they compared cannabis to heroin and cocaine, subjecting its use to the same severe penalties. This had actually made the passing of a federal law pointless, if not for extending the prohibition of the plant also to the therapeutic and industrial uses.

Drugs in Geneva, he refused to sign the final version because he considered the Convention too weak.

As he declared himself almost twenty years later, in fact, the convention proposal, even though it included flowers and resins obtained from cannabis in the list of substances whose trade was prohibited, did not prohibit the cultivation and spread of every part of the plant and focused only on her doping parts[42].

The first battle was therefore lost, but the prohibitionist bureaucrat was already working on drafting the law to be passed in the US Senate. On 14 January 1937 he summoned the Federal Bureau of Narcotics. It was discussed which parts of the plant should be banned and, while his collaborators insisted on explaining how marijuana was obtainable only from flowers and to a lesser extent from leaves, Anslinger proved inflexible in his stance and insisted that any cultivation and use of any part of the Hemp plant was to be banned.

The full transcription of the meeting is available thanks to congressional archives and reading some of its passages is enlightening[43]. When they pointed out to him that not all varieties of Hemp existing in nature are suitable to develop the stimulating principle[44], Anslinger replied that it would be too dangerous to make distinctions, and that an all-inclusive definition was needed. When they objected that, according to the analysis, the drug was obtainable only from flower sand leaves, and not from the whole plant, he merely dismissed the argument stating that they were details that could have confused police officers. Astonished by this, they asked him if he intended to ban even the seeds, which were used across the country as feed for birds. Unmoved, he replied that banning the seed served as a preventive measure and resolved problems at the source. When, finally, they reminded him that that plant was an

---

[42] H.J. Anslinger, W.F. Tompkins, *The Traffic in Narcotics*, Funk & Wagnalls Company, 1953.

[43] The full transcript of the discussion is available in English at: http://www.druglibrary.net/schaffer/Hemp/taxact/canncon.htm

[44] At the time of the events, the chemical composition of cannabis was still unknown. THC was first identified and studied by the researchers Raphael Mechoulam, Yechiel Gaoni and Habib Edery of the Weizmann Institute, Israel, 1964.

integral part of many medicines regularly on the market, he retorted with a disarming: "I was surprised to hear some medical experts at Geneva recently say that is has absolutely no medical use!".

A humiliation to a millennium of history, research, culture and tradition.

Anslinger himself, along with some officials of Treasury Secretary Andrew Mellon, worked on the draft to be submitted to Congress. The idea was not to explicitly ban cannabis, but to pass a "prohibitive tax". A prohibition masquerading as a fiscal measure. A procedure that in the United States of those years was adopted when there was the possibility of ending in an excessive debate that could compromise the adoption of a text[45]. The proposal was renamed the "Marijuana Tax Act" and stated that every person who sells, acquires, dispenses, or possesses marijuana must register to the Internal Revenue Service and pay a US$24 registration fee per year[46], as well as pay a US$1 tax on each ounce of product transported or sold. The first article of the Act also specified what should be defined as "marijuana", and was therefore subject to the new tax regime:

> *The term "marijuana" means all parts of the plant Cannabis Sativa L., whether growing or not; the seeds thereof; the resin extracted from any part of such plant; and every compound, manufacture, salt, derivative, mixture, or preparation of such plant, its seeds, or resin.*

A dollar of the time is over US$17 today, while one ounce is 28.35 grams. It means that a Hemp fiber manufacturer for textile use would have to pay the equivalent of today's US$60,000 in taxes for every hundred kilos of product. Nonsense.

---

[45] An example of a "prohibitive tax" is the National Firearms Act, approved in 1934. It formally kept allowing the sale of firearms, but in substance it made it unworkable by establishing that each transaction was subject to a fee of two hundred dollars.

[46] US$24 in 1937 equaled to US$424 in 2017 according to historical conversion tables.

On the surface the law didn't target its therapeutical uses, subjecting doctors only to the registry fee; however the check-ups and possible penalties against them were evidently designed to sink this sector too. Every time a doctor prescribed a compound containing cannabis, he had immediately to communicate to the Federal Bureau of Narcotics the name and address of the patient, nature of the disease, dosage and prescribed quantities; each recipe then had to be registered and stored for two years, during which the narcotics agents could have carried out inspections. Any violation of the law would have been punished with imprisonment of up to five years and fines of up to US$2,000 dollars, the same penalty for everyone, and for whatever reason, violating the *Marijuana Tax Act.*

It's not hard to figure how a law written that way amounted to a real prohibition, making the handling of Hemp too risky for anyone. It was evident also to many insiders. The Secretary of the National Oil Seed Institute stated bluntly that the law would kill the large Hemp industry. While the spokesman of the American Medical Association (AMA), William Woodward, accused the committee led by Anslinger of having worked in secret for two years, without involving the doctors in their intention to "outlaw a medicine such as cannabis, a substance used in America in complete safety and for various diseases for over a hundred years"[47].

Within a few weeks, the proposal was presented to Congress as a simple measure aimed at freeing the streets of America from demonic murder smoke. None of the trade representatives against the measure was invited to speak and soon after, they got to the vote. On 11 May 1937, the Senate approved the Marijuana Tax Act, signed by President Roosevelt on 2 August, and entered into force two months later.

1 October 1937.

After centuries of development and progress, the history of Hemp underwent a radical reversal of course. The despicable era of prohibition began.

---

[47] Herer J., *The Emperor wears no clothes* sop. Cit.

Chapter 7

DOLCE VITA

February 2005. After the sack from the Dutch, my business activity went through an unexpected boost: the profitable era of independent projects began.

I'm almost 22 years old and I feel like a volcano ready to explode. Lots of ideas, energies, projects. Zero economic resources to make them happen. But I'm determined to get them done and my belief is stronger than any obstacle. I'm sure I can make my dreams come true. Someone might call it the "law of attraction". I feel bold, therefore lucky.

I take a low-cost flight to Barcelona, and once there I get a bed in the dorm of a super cheap hostel, to participate to the second edition of *Spannabis*, what has now become the world biggest cannabis expo. Here I propose to various exhibiting companies advertising spaces in the forthcoming *Magical Italy*, explaining to them the great possibilities for growth in the Italian market. I sell all the main pages and go back home after a weekend of full immersion with €4000 of advance payments in cash. It's the beginning of my editorial cannabusiness. I become a Stakhanovite, I put the utmost attention into everything I do and leave nothing to chance. I feel like it's a climax and I want to play my cards at my best.

A month later, on 19-20 March, *Cannabis Tipo Forte* takes place near Pistoia, the very first Italian Hemp fair, hosted by my friend Dr. Cinquini, who I helped in the organization of it after the visit to Versilia.

To call it "fair" would be a nice compliment: it is, in fact, a pavilion inside another event, where a dozen fearless exhibitors present themselves to the public for the first time. The visitors are few and above all, very skeptical. But all this has little relevance: the event represents an important turning point and opens the door to future, larger and more structured events.

Hemp, an incredible story

Here I have the pleasure of meeting Scott Blakey for the first time, better known as Shantibaba, a person of rare caliber, breeder[48] of international fame and father of some historical varieties with countless awards, including the mythical *White Widow*.

These are intense days of meetings and contacts, of turmoil and opportunities. A great new project is sprouting.

I returned back home by car with Jack, a friend already active in the industry for a few years and owner of one of the first Italian growing shops near Milan.

The lights of the cars lit up the street, it was about ten o'clock in the evening and Jack was driving slowly.

We were close to Pistoia, returning from the first Italian fair dedicated to Hemp - Cannabis Tipo Forte 2005 *– where we participated with the stand of Enjoint. We were returning to Milan after the two days of exhibition, and I was particularly excited that* Stampa Alternativa *was very interested in my project.*

I also began thinking about a possible new magazine dedicated to alternative lifestyles (therefore talking not only about Hemp but also about other topics) just few weeks earlier, precisely, when I was "kindly invited" to leave my position of editor-in-chief for reasons that I like to call "of communicative order". To tell the truth, the idea of realizing such a publication has been going around my mind for several years: it was one of my many secrets wishes that I never dare to realize because I knew how utopian it was. It was mixed with many others, like playing in the NBA, making a concert with Caparezza or a theatrical show with Beppe Grillo, opening a coffee-shop in Italy, spending a night (what an overstatement! an hour) with Manuela Arcuri, etc. Then I decided, I chose the least insane dream and, strong of a short but intense editorial experience, I gave it a shot. It took just a couple of meetings, a few phone calls and a few hours in front of the

---

[48] Selector of cannabis seeds strains.

computer to realize that it would have a good following. The "magazine" project was slowly taking shape; I now knew that an important publishing house was interested in it and other people came forward to support the cause. It was not just a vision anymore and, even if it had only been such, it was at least of a shared vision.

That evening with Jack, we talked about the Fair we just attended, of the people we met and of how strong their Hemp biscuits were. We laughed, recalling expressions or phrases from the previous days. We both had issues to deal with, and worries in which to lose ourselves, but that was not the right moment for it.

A few weeks later the Bern fair would have taken place - The CannaTrade *- and we had to prepare everything, given that we would have a stand there too. I realized that it was certainly not the quietest time for starting a project like the magazine, but I also knew that, if we hadn't done it soon, I would have risked watching it fade away.*

It often happens like that: an idea is born, it is welcomed with general enthusiasm, the first problems come by, and you easily give up. Often, but not always; and this time it wouldn't happen: we were determined and we already had in mind what to do. Soon we had to propose the project to various sponsors, contact new editors and make the first official documents, we could no longer wait: we had to find a name for the magazine, soon!

We needed something in Italian, inherent to the topic, a winning, classic, symbolic name, easy to remember, serious but not too much, composed at most of two words, not too long but not too short, not trivial but not complicated, without political or religious references and, possibly, stylish.

I was a little worried, I had no idea and all these details disoriented me. Given the playful circumstances, and the beer that was beginning to be felt, we began shooting

Hemp, an incredible story

out a series of absurd and meaningless proposals, names that we could never have used, useless names.

A few minutes later, suddenly, the lighting.

"Jack, I found it!"

It was perfect, perhaps the best you could find, as spontaneous and magical as love at first sight. If I were to romanticize the moment even further, I would say that, looking at the stars, I saw the name traced in the sky.

Anyway, I communicated it to the other partners; they liked the name straight away, which was not to be taken for granted.

That night I happily fell asleep, dreaming of the NBA, the coffee-shop in Italy and Manuela Arcuri.

I was happy because a dream had come true: Dolce Vita (Sweet Life) was born.

From that moment onward I dedicate my body and soul to it. And the above passage was the first edition of "Looking at the stars", my column in the magazine.

At the end of March 2005, in Pantelleria, a 23-year-old boy named Joseph hanged himself after being arrested for possession of marijuana. I was enraged! I launched the initiative "murderous prohibition" both on the web and by printing and distributing thousands of flyers. My mission is to inform as many people as possible that this made no sense. I realize that *Dolce Vita* can be an incredible mouthpiece.

Among the magazine's early supporters is Filippo Vona, known as Filo Green, a run-down activist, warrior of modern times, an expert grower and owner of one of the first growing shops in Italy, in Rome. Thanks to him, I came into contact with the Roman publishing house Stampa Alternativa, with which we organize a meeting. They liked the project, but they are particularly meticulous and think a little too old-fashioned for my liking. They have a lot of experience in the industry and as a result they have seen it all already, including careless kids with far-fetched ideas lasting a few months and then dissolving into nothing, leaving debts. I'm told that to set up a bimonthly national distribution, like what I had in mind, about €100,000 were needed. I replied that I had about €100 in my bank account. The "thousands" were missing. We drop it waiting for future updates, but neither them nor I are very convinced of the collaboration.

In early April, I go to Bern to attend *CannaTrade* - already at its fifth edition and one of the best in Europe, if not the best. I only have in my hand a draft of the cover of the first issue of *Dolce Vita*, inspired by the poster of Fellini's legendary film, on which Anita Ekberg appears. A simple color A4 sheet that I printed at home is all I have to show potential sponsors and partners. Along with this, I have only my words – in a scholastic and macaronic English – to try to convince them of the value of the project.

I sell €40,000 of advertising space in three days. Half a miracle. It will be the economic basis on which to build *Dolce Vita* and the necessary funds for the first year of publications. "Fuck it, I made it!" I think to myself, knowing well, however, the bulk of responsibilities that I have taken on.

It's curious to see how some of the investors don't realize at all who is behind this. I introduce myself to everyone as the creator and author of the nascent magazine – I have nothing to hide –but from the looks I receive, it is clear that few believed me.

A swaggering little boy in his twenties can be the editor and at the same time the person who goes to propose advertising spaces?

Here, I also have the opportunity to meet Howard Marks in person, the mythical *Mr. Nice* of the book I read a few years earlier during an English period. We have a chat, take a picture together and he signs an inscription.

"Is it all true or am I living inside a movie?"

A question that would repeat in those incredible years.

10 April 2005 - Pope Wojtyla dies.

I lock myself in the house for few months and become a hermit. I work twenty-five hours a day on *Dolce Vita*, from content to logistics and bureaucracy. For the beginning of summer everything must be ready

Hemp, an incredible story

– and so it will be. After several negotiations, I come to a provisional agreement with *Stampa Alternativa*, and I have the honor of having their founder Marcello Baraghini as Director in charge of the first issue. He himself writes the first editorial, under which we publish a picture of him from 1993 together with Albert Hofmann, the Swiss scientist who discovered LSD.

Baraghini is a historical editor: he is the creator of the series *Millelire*, small books that in the 90s revolutionized the industry, selling as much as twenty million copies. But above all, Baraghini is a legendary activist. Friend of Marco Pannella, already by the 1970s he published the *Manual for the cultivation of Marijuana* and his editorial counter-information initiatives caused one hundred and twenty-seven complaints – and an on-the-run experience – all related to thoughtcrime. A true purple heart of this profession, in our nation and in those times.

So at the end of June 2005, the first issue of *Dolce Vita* goes to print. I put a piece of my heart into it and I feel exhausted when I finally send the files for layout, but I'm more than satisfied. Forty-eight pages, twenty thousand copies and no cover price, which means free distribution. At the suggestion of my lawyer I insert the caption "adult magazine", which I do not like the thought of, and in fact will be removed from the next edition.

The subtitle is "Alternative lifestyles" and the other taglines on the cover are: "In/outdoor cultivation, Therapeutic, textiles and industrial Cannabis, Product reviews, Ethnobotanic, Trade and events reports, Jurisprudence and laws, News from the world, Photos and comics, Music, books and movies, Sports and travel, Thoughts and words". A lot of stuff, for a great issue! Newborn but already well defined, with some new contributors and others very well known, especially in the world of cannabis. In about ten days it will be ready, then it will need to be shown, distributed, and promoted.

I take a deep breath and take the chance to buy my first motorized vehicle: a white Renault Master van from 1987 without power steering and with a semi-sampled closed trunk equipped with two folding cots and a water tank. To tour Milan with it is a challenge, parking it is even harder. But the idea of spending summer as a tramp, sleeping where I want is irresistible; and I also combine business with pleasure, knowing that it could be useful for work.

I have the brilliant idea of customizing the sides and the bonnet with the *Enjoint* logo which includes three icons depicting the peace symbol, a heart and an unmistakable marijuana leaf. It all guarantees me constant attention from traffic police, who do not hesitate to stop me at every opportunity. It's too hard trying to explain them that if I had weed or if I had the intention to breaking any law, I certainly wouldn't go around in a van like that.

Returning from Switzerland, at the Chiasso border, the customs officers suddenly stand up as they see me coming, as if they spotted Pablo Escobar. They take apart my vehicle and for about three hours, they check every single corner of my luggage and goods, without finding anything illegal. At the same time, I witness a parade of dark high-profile cars, with tinted windows, led by distinct gentlemen in suits, crossing the border without the slightest control. Certainly, all good people, for heaven's sake! The potential criminal is me who have a ganja leaf on the bonnet of an old van.

But the inconveniences are compensated by the approval of other drivers who wherever I go, while overtaking me, sound their horn and raise their thumbs, amid great smiles and incitements. People love this plant!

The first issue of *Dolce Vita* is ready and the first time I leaf through it I have shivers all over my body. It's a dream come true. Certainly, it had its imperfections, but the journey is long and the margins for improvement are infinite.

I go back to the *Rototom Sunsplash*, the great reggae festival in the province of Udine, but this time, as an exhibitor with my own stand to show the magazine. Within the lapse of two summers, my interests have completely changed. Getting high no longer falls between them and my passion for Hemp now finds space on the pages of a new beautiful publication. *Dolce Vita* gets a great reception, it is a revolving door of people who come to pick up their copy; many give me compliments, ask for information, and want to subscribe. Walking around the park and seeing families sitting on the lawns reading the magazine with interest and attention is a great feeling.

I spend the summer wandering around Italian shores with a couple of friends and the super van. We sleep on the seaside, in the city centers, in abusive parking lots and wherever it happens. When we can't find a place in the shade, in the morning we get waken up by the heat, it's a scorcher.

In Lignano, at dawn, we hear a loud knock on the bonnet, imagining an angry officer with a fine in his hand. We open up and see a boy with the face of one who had been exposed to various after hour activities and who knows what else. He looks at us and asks, "Do you happen to sell weed? Are you like home delivery?" We shut the doors without even answering him.

At that time websites like Mariuana.it broke out: Semini.it, Shop.mariuana.it and, indeed, Mariuana.it are subjected to seizure by the Postal Police and the owner of the three websites is arrested because he is considered to be the head of a criminal organization dedicated to drug dealing.

I personally write a long communiqué that I publish on *Enjoint* and in issue one of *Dolce Vita*, in which I try to respond to the lies that have appeared on national media, recalling in particular how the sale of cannabis seeds in Italy is completely legal and therefore any illegal use of such seeds is the responsibility of those who buy them, not those who sell them. I close the article with these words:

> *While throughout Europe the various states admit the failure of prohibition and opt for a more tolerant approach, here in Italy the climate of persecution and rage toward the almost four million consumers continues. [...] All our solidarity goes out to the people involved in this crazy operation. This is our message to make them understand that we are here and that from here we will not move. We will continue to do what we have always done, head-on, because...RIGHT OR WRONG, IT CAN'T BE A CRIME.*

This is one of our first concrete actions of counter-information and "editorial anti-prohibition". The communiqué is taken up by various websites and newspapers. The owner of Mariuana.it will then be acquitted, years later, but forced to pay thousands of Euros for his defense in an endless series of criminal proceedings, lawyers and administrative fines. He will eventually close his websites.

After this episode I consider the hypothesis of moving the server of *Enjoint* abroad, in the Netherlands, to safeguard myself but above all, the community users.

It's a busy summer for me too, focused on *Dolce Vita* and working assiduously for the next issue, scheduled for the autumn.

With Stampa Alternativa we come one step away from the definitive agreement, but eventually I pull back. I fear that the project will be distorted. Besides, I want to hold on control, now that the boat has sailed, and I think I can do it on my own.

I solve the bureaucratic part by relying on a Swiss journalist, hence the magazine's temporarily legal address becomes Bellinzona, in Canton Ticino. In this way I can get around the norm, born in the fascist era and not yet set aside, which imposes on any Italian periodic publication the registration in court with a responsible director registered in the Register of Journalists. In the rest of Europe, none of this exists.

I also begin to better structure the editorial staff, entrusting the graphics to a professional and involving new collaborators. In the end, taking away the expenses, what remains in my pocket is derisory, almost nothing. But I am convinced that it is the right move to invest all available resources toward the growth of the magazine.

It's now October, and the next issue of *Dolce Vita* is ready. This is what I write in my column:

> *I like to think I'm on the right track. Aware of our fragility, but optimistic about our present and future. I light the candles with a light but decisive blow. I drink the last sip of tea, now tepid... and I'm leaving! I loosen the moorings and open the sails; the wind fills them up. I take off leaving behind clouds and storms. In front of me only the ocean. I know it will be a long and difficult journey.*

But in the end, I'll get somewhere. I'm exhausted, but I smile... because I can still dream.

Chapter 8

WAR ON DRUGS

The menacing ship of prohibition had thought to untie the moorings and open the sails seventy years before officially sailing, as we saw, on 1 October 1937.

A bunch of politicians, journalists, judges and cops were the crew, and tons of fibs spread through the press served as fuel. In reality, if prohibition had really been a boat, it would have been large enough to make the big cruises that today assault the Venice lagoon to the edge of the square of St. Mark look tiny. Its exhausts would emit black and gross fumes, such as the interests of the oil companies they defend. Its passage would leave a permanent trail of plastic waste of all kinds, such as those produced by the Du Pont family. But in 1937 prohibition, although supported by great interests, was still a small boat, to the point that someone, perhaps realizing the damage it would cause, tried to overthrow it while still in the wharf.

That someone was called Fiorello Enrico La Guardia, son of a musician, who arrived in the United States from Cerignola, Puglia. With his name Americanized to Henry, La Guardia became Mayor of New York in 1934, soon building a reputation as a man of honor, strongly against corruption and crime. He wasn't an anti-prohibitionist, and it is believed he never used Cannabis: he was still a white man of the 1930s, moreover his political views were conservative in the characteristic of the Republican Party. However, the story of marijuana as an absolute evil and generator of all violence just didn't sound right to him, and he was even less convinced by the scientific level of studies that Anslinger used to justify its prohibition.

To see straight, La Guardia summoned the scientists of the New York Academy of Medicine and appointed a specialized commission to produce a study on the medical, psychiatric and social effects of marijuana consumption, starting in Harlem, where cannabis was quite widespread within the Black community. The research lasted until 1944, when the results were published[49], summarized in thirteen points, the most relevant of which certified that:

- The practice of smoking marijuana did not lead to addiction in the medical sense of the word.
- The use of marijuana did not lead to morphine or heroin or cocaine addiction.
- Marijuana is not the determining factor in the commission of major crimes.
- Juvenile delinquency is not associated with the practice of smoking marijuana.

The thirteenth and final point summed it all up in a blunt and definitive sentence:

- The publicity concerning the catastrophic effects of marijuana smoking in New York City is unfounded[50].

No wonder the American press, beginning with that of William Hearst, chose not to emphasize the research. Harry Anslinger, for his part, did not take well this meddling of science in its dozen yearlong activity dedicated to the criminalization of the Hemp plant. Firstly, he threw up a statement with tones dictated directly by his anger, defining the La Guardia report "inappropriate, superficial and false", then issued a circular aimed at all doctors, scientists and researchers of America to warn them that no other research on marijuana would be tolerated, if not directly requested and commissioned by the Federal Bureau of Narcotics

While the La Guardia report was still being drafted, even the American Doctors Association returned to charge, with an editorial published in the association's newspaper in December 1942, in which they cried out for the recognition of cannabis' benefits in the treatment of depression, inappetence and opioid addiction. As had been clear from the start, indeed the Marijuana Tax Act allowed only in theory the

---

[49] *Mayor's Committee on Marihuana, by The New York Academy of Medicine, The La Guardia Committee Report – The Marijuana Problem in the City of New York*, City of New York, 1944.

[50] The full report is available at: http://www.druglibrary.net/schaffer/Library/studies/lag/lagmenu.htm

prescription of medicines taken from the plant, but from a practical point of view things were very different. Only in 1939 – just to put things straight – the agents of the Bureau handcuffed more than three thousand doctors, guilty of having committed alleged violations to the law[51]; and repression continued until 1942, when all cannabis-based medicines were removed from the official pharmacopoeia of the United States. In the long run, Anslinger's brutal attack against anyone who dared to raise doubts about his law brought the desired results.

La Guardia ended his third and final term as Mayor of New York City in 1945 and, now ill, retired to private life. The American Medical Association, on the other hand, which still needed federal funds to continue to exist, quickly and definitively returned into line, announcing its own heel-turn in an editorial in April 1945 in which it completely disproved the convictions expressed until the day before and invited the government and the federal agents to "consider marijuana a threat wherever it is present"[52].

From the desk of the Federal Bureau of Narcotics, Anslinger, *Deus ex machina* of prohibition, commissioned an increasingly large team of guards who every day carried out stings, usually in Black neighborhoods, search for cannabis smokers to be thrown in prison. But he wasn't satisfied. American law was still too permissive for his taste and, above all, in the rest of the world cannabis was not as yet recognized as a problem.

If the war on Hemp in the United States could be considered won, Harry Anslinger began to aim for exporting the law. The ship of prohibition was ready to set sail, now for real, to conquer the ports of half the world.

The 1950s were the years of the "Truman doctrine", that is the theory of a world divided into two blocs, whose citizens soon learned to familiarize themselves with the term "Cold War" to define the relations between East and West, dividing the portion of the world led by Moscow on one side, and Washington's allies on the other. Communism

---

[51] Grinspoon L., *Marijuana reconsidered*, Harvard University Press, 1971.

[52] *Marijuana Problems*, in Journal of the American Medical Association, n. 17, 28 April 1945.

was the new bogeyman of an America that evidently always needed an enemy to be fought, be it real or presumed.

The Bureau followed suit and, in order to be able to link marijuana to the new monster that was occupying the papers, did not hesitate to overturn completely the theory that they had used to invoke the repression of the plant that haunted Anslinger and his sponsors. Previously weed was "murder smoke", pushing the consumer to cut and stab, beat and shoot. Now the head of the Narcotics Bureau, with the same unwavering and fraudulent certainty, asserts:

> *Marijuana renders its users not violent at all, but so peaceful – and pacifistic! – [...] Communists could and would sell Marijuana to American boys to sap their will to fight – to make us a nation of zombie pacifists*[53].

In this way, helped as always by a complacent media, he convinced the public that the Marijuana Tax Act of 1937 needed a reinforcement. For the security of the country, it was necessary to approve even more restrictive laws and fight the war on cannabis all over the globe.

In December 1951, U.S. President Harry Truman signed the much-invoked act. The Marijuana Tax Act was amended with new restrictive articles, including the automatic and mandatory prison sentences for every cannabis consumer. The punishments were draconian: two years of prison for the first time you were caught, even with a single joint, five years the second time, and ten from the third onwards.

In 1954, the World Health Organization also bowed to the will of Stars and Stripes. Millennia of practices by half the world's people, the studies of ancient Chinese medicine, the pioneers of modern medicine in the nineteenth century, fifty or more diseases against which cannabis was recommended just thirty years earlier: all this work completely erased. The official document of the 12 July 1954 sentenced:

> *There is no scientific justification for the use of cannabis in medicine [...] Cannabis drugs are generally*

---

[53] Herer J., *The Emperor wears no clothes* Op. cit.

> *regarded as obsolete [...] this practice needs to be permanently replaced by the medical use of opioid drugs*[54].
>
> *Not even a year had passed and a new WHO report made things even worse, emphasizing the danger of cannabis:*
>
> *"from every point of view, whether physical, social, mental or criminological.*
>
> *[...] requesting governments to take measures to suppress domestic Cannabis consumption*[55].

It was the first victory of prohibition in the international arena, and above all, it was the assist that Anslinger was waiting for in view of the UN conference, scheduled for 1961, in which the United States had to decide on common policies on drugs.

At this meeting the United States, obviously represented by Anslinger himself, toppled on the table their weight of hegemonic power, getting more or less everything they wanted. A special treatment was given to Hemp, equal to that of heroin. Not only was it inserted into Schedule I, i.e. the list of the most harmful drugs, those that "gave addiction and presented a serious risk of abuse", but, unlike other heavy substances such as cocaine, it was also catalogued in Schedule IV, i.e. the list of drugs with "zero or extremely low therapeutic value".

The 1961 Convention committed all UN Member States to pass national laws as soon as possible with the aim to repress the "cultivation, production, extraction, preparation, possession, sale, distribution, purchase, shipping, transport, import and export" of any substance included in the list.

Now the war on Hemp had begun all over the world!

Anslinger's ideas about marijuana as a weapon of the demon Communist Party to intoxicate the population broke through

---

[54] *UN Economic and Social Council, Resolution* 548 FI (XVIII), 12 July 1954.

[55] M. Osbeck, H. Bromberg, *Marijuana Law in a Nutshell*, West Academic Publishing, 2017.

everywhere. In socialist countries the same result was achieved, reversing the plot: there, in fact, cannabis was criminalized being a deceitful instrument of a capitalist conspiracy aimed at quelling out the virtues of young Soviets.

In the decade that followed, countries around the world seemed to challenge each other as to who could make the most repressive law, trying to outdo the example set by the US.

Europe stuck to the imposed orders without any particular creativity, approving laws that reserved for the possession of cannabis the same penalties as for the most harmful drugs, including prison. Jail time was expected not only for smuggling, but also for simple consumption. But at other latitudes, inhumane and frightening laws were issued: several nations determined that law enforcement bodies could forcibly subject every citizen to random urine tests to verify the use of cannabis, proceeding with the arrest in a case of positivity. In Saudi Arabia and Singapore, "Middle Ages" standards were adopted: those who were found in possession of a joint, even a single one, were condemned to caning in public. In China the use of every drug was not considered a criminal offence, but the outcome was even worse. Maoists considered it a disease to be treated through an indefinite stay in the laogai, the infamous "re-education and work camp". In other countries – and they were not few – the death penalty was applied, through hanging, beheading or shooting, not only for drug smuggling, but also for the possession of a few grams; this is still the case in Indonesia and Malaysia.

The United Nations, which a few years earlier had approved with great pomp the Universal Declaration of Human Rights, had nothing to say.

Everywhere in the world prisons began to fill with citizens who had committed no crime but selling or even just smoking the dried flowers of a plant. Naturally, as with any prohibition policy, consumption did not decrease, but on the contrary grew out of proportion, with the criminal cartels making tons of profit by controlling the illegal trade.

In 1962, at the age of 70, thirty-two of which he passed fighting Hemp, Harry Jacob Anslinger put his resignation in the hands of new President John F. Kennedy, retreating to private life. In time, he saw himself on the big screen, played by Oscar winner Edmond O'Brien in the movie Lucky Luciano by the Italian director Francesco Rosi. He spent his final years in his native Pennsylvania, complacently observing his own creation, the prohibition, which followed the course he planned and only grew over time.

Chapter 9

YOU REAP WHAT YOU SOW

The path for *Dolce Vita* is set: issue after issue my leadership is more confident, my work more relaxed. I know there's still a lot to say about the world of Hemp and, above all, there is so much to do.

Friends and acquaintances are amazed at how you can fill the pages with articles about a topic that seems so specific.

"How can you have so much to write about marijuana?" they ask.

And to each of them I reply by giving them a copy of the magazine.

The deeper I delve into the Hemp topic, the more I'm fascinated by it and the more I realize how much there is to be told about this precious resource. One could write hundreds of books on its therapeutic uses alone, not to mention the industrial ones. If we then were to approach its spiritual, religious, recreational and playful uses, all the paper of in the world would not be enough to contain all Hemp-related stories, notions, news and information.

But *Dolce Vita* is not just about cannabis and years later I'll realize how important the choice made in those first editions not to limit it to a single topic, albeit a broad one, was. The subtitle, *Alternative lifestyles*, represents its connotation in an effective and synthetic way.

In issue one, we publish an article by Marco Matiuzzo, freelance journalist, titled *Supermarket super-ethic* which talks about critical consumption, social and environmental responsibility. Topics that are extremely current today around the world, were much less so in Italy in October 2005. The article explains what boycotting is and talks of the first actions of this kind against multinationals. A few pages further and another important article is *How to use psychedelics without getting hurt* by Gilberto Camilla, president of the Italian Society for the Study on States of Consciousness. Counter-information, strategies for containing damage, topics considered taboo by public opinion: *Dolce Vita* is also focused on this.

The editorial line is, of course, very influenced by my personal experiences: if I had had the chance to read an article like Camilla's years earlier maybe I would have avoided certain idiocies; and that's why now, with a similar channel at my disposal, I feel a responsibility to offer a useful service to younger generations. Prohibition is of no use, on the contrary, it creates even more attraction. Information and education are the ways to achieve concrete results.

On the magazine's official manifesto, which we publish on its website, I insert this important pitch:

> *Dolce Vita does not take any position on the use of drugs (whatever they may be) but limits itself to providing the right information about it, inviting everyone to a personal responsibility and an eventual conscious experimentation.*

It is one of the foundations on which our entire activity is and will be based.

In the meantime, the staff is defined, and the shake-down period is over. Nonetheless, I still find myself, together with the graphic designer, working extra hours to close each issue on time, meeting the deadlines. We make the final corrections in my apartment in Milan, in a *tour de force* fueled by cigarettes and coffee that keep us going till three or four in the morning. But there is much satisfaction and this pays off all our efforts. Each page is made with passion and with the greatest possible care.

It is December 2005, the issue number two of *Dolce Vita* is almost ready, only my column is missing. I run away from the city and retire for few days in the heart of the Dolomites, where I was born and raised, and I write these lines:

> *With all this cold, in the midst of this biting wind, it would be almost permissible to feel alone and desolate... but instead I feel light, relieved and protected from all this poetry that surrounds me. And in this splendid waiting, in this sweet hibernation, I enjoy this magical winter.*

Words that seem written by a wise and balanced person. In reality I'm still full of rubbish and arrogance, typical of a twenty-two-year-old. And to confirm that, I spend that New Year's Eve together with a friend of mine in Ibiza, where first I risk to being arrested in the historic nightclub Pacha, and then I get into serious trouble in the Gypsy neighborhood. But in the end, I return home safe and sound.

In February 2006, the shameful Fini-Giovanardi law is approved, equating light and heavy drugs. Making a fifty-year step back, Italy suddenly becomes the strictest European nation when it comes to drugs, while the rest of the world opens up to policies of tolerance and regularization, especially with regard to cannabis. It is a nefarious law that ruins the lives of thousands of harmless consumers before being rejected by the Constitutional Court years later.

Dolce Vita gathers consensus both among readers and the companies of the sector. It is important to give it continuity and respect the schedule. More than the collection and organization of content, the greater commitment during this period is about bureaucratic issues and above all balancing the books.

The solution of the provisional headquarters in Bellinzona did not prove to be ideal, and the costs are prohibitive. I'm at a dead end. Publishing a magazine without neither an official registration nor a director enrolled in the Register of Journalists would constitute an "illegal press" crime, something I would like to avoid. So, I decide to gamble, and issue number three comes out with a mailbox from Amsterdam listed as the editorial address and Mr. Wolff's Blankers as director. I wonder if such a person ever existed...

It then looked like a magazine printed and distributed in Italy but based abroad. Could it be done? I have no idea, but at the moment that's my only option, so I decide to proceed anyway. It is what it is. Our distribution currently only takes place through fifty grow shops, community centers and events, so we are not yet particularly exposed.

The new issue has a beautiful cover dedicated to the Fini-Giovanardi law that bears the slogan *Witch hunt of new law on drugs*, and then some blurbs about the interview with Caparezza, the protest of the No-Tav[56], the phenomenon of Salvia Divinorum.

I'm starting to feel good. I'm leaving behind demons and troubles, and I'm finding my balance. I'm growing up. In my diary I write:

> Planet Earth. It's April of the year 2006 of the current Era. Italy.
>
> Highlights: Thomas – the kidnapped child that became a main media event – is found, dead. The culprits are in jail.
>
> Provenzano, mafia boss of bosses, fugitive for forty years, has been arrested. The democrats won the election. Iraq and the Middle East are still hit by riots, wars, ...
>
> Summer is coming and you can feel it, the days are getting longer and warmer. And I live. What else could I do?

The *Dolce Vita* story goes through a twist. Through my Roman friend Filippo Vona, I get in contact with Fabrizio Rondolino – an established journalist and television author, spokesman for the PM D'Alema during his time in government but, above all, a convinced and determined anti-prohibitionist – who agrees in giving us his signature and holding the role of responsible director so that ours becomes in all respect a "true" magazine. Thanks to this, I can proceed with the registration of the magazine at the Court of Milan, where it gets officially registered on 3 May 2006. The collaboration with Rondolino is free from any diktat and he'll never put his nose in any content, leaving to myself the management of the editorial line. I do ask him to write some articles of politics and current affairs in a column titled *Critical Point* for us though. His support is important, given in return of only a sincere thank you.

In the fourth issue of *Dolce Vita* we publish for the first time an article that talks about vaporizers, a new tool that allows the consumption of cannabis avoiding combustion, and thus eliminating in full the damage

---

[56] High speed train

by harmful substances through the smoking process. A real revolution in the world of therapeutic cannabis begins.

It's June 2006, *Dolce Vita* turns one year old. From the first issue till now we have distributed seventy thousand copies, overcoming adversities and obstacles that we thought were insuperable. We started without a publishing house, without the necessary budget for such a project and without professional editors.

Passion, determination, courage and willpower have accompanied us from day one; we have experimented, improvised and sometimes even gambled, but it was worth it. That's right!

Step by step we have grown, we have become publishers, we have found collaborations, supporters, journalists excited to participate to our project and, above all, we have won the trust of our readers and sponsors. *Dolce Vita* is now a solid reality, officially registered in court and available throughout Italy from over one hundred and twenty distribution points.

But we still have a lot to improve. And the goal for the new editorial year is to grow further, to get to newsstands, print as many pages and copies as possible because in our opinion this is much more than just a magazine.

Enjoint also grows and becomes an online landmark for Italian growers, a virtual family that shares interests and passions.

Meanwhile the fair *Cannabis Strong Type* moves to Bologna for its second iteration and it manages to make big numbers, earning a place among the European trade fairs in the sector. More than five thousand visitors, journalists, politicians, specialists, but also some casual curious crowds participate in conferences and meetings dedicated to medical cannabis, cultivation and drug policies.

I turn twenty-three. In Milan I get to know a person who I will call Mimmo to guarantee him due privacy. He's a hyperactive boy, loves partying, is a few years older than me, full of knowledge, and countless ideas. We immediately get along with each other and become companions. He takes me to some cool parties in the Lombardy capital, some in avantgarde premises, others in private houses. There we find flowing *the White, the Snow, the bomb* ... or more simply cocaine.

On weekends Mimmo and I are inseparable, the nights become longer and the pupils of those who snort the fatal white powder smaller. And in Milan, in those habitats, it's the normality. You trick yourself into thinking you're having fun, of feeling good for real, of living at another level, at the top. But it's just rubbish for losers. Nothing more.

But Mimmo also introduces me to a lot of interesting people and so I end up at J-Ax's birthday party, the top Italian rapper of the time, in a club with a few dozen of his friends, among celebrities and common people. The group Article 31 recently fell apart and Ax is trying to reinvent himself amid a thousand difficulties. I'm impressed by his humility and simplicity, unlike other characters from the world of music and entertainment that I got to know in this period and that I utterly disdain.

It is the summer of the World Cup, with Zidane's header at Materazzi, the "World Champions" screamed for four consecutive times yelled by our commentator at end of the game, the "po-po-po" refrain on the Seven Nation Army by The White Stripes, and the squares full of partying people.

The nights out with Mimmo continue and we have a few of them along with Guè Pequeno and other members of the *Dogo Gang*, a renowned crew of Milanese rappers. Club Dogo's new album *Penna Capitale* has just been released and everyone in the city talks about it. We enter in clubs skipping the queues, between girls in ecstasy and complacent bouncers, we end up in the VIP room, and we do not pay a cent. It's all very cool but I feel like I'm not in the right place, that this way of living is not for me. After a few months I distance myself, while still maintaining contact and good relations with everyone.

I fly to Rome to develop some important initiatives related to *Dolce Vita* and to understand if the conditions are right for bringing the magazine to newsstands.

Between a meeting and a business appointment, the contact that is taking me around the capital says he has to do a little detour, "just for a few minutes." And without even realizing it I find myself in the elevator of a degraded apartment along with him and another guy that I've never seen before, who was carrying two bulky suitcases with the unmistakable smell of marijuana. We enter an apartment on the seventh floor, where immediately the content of the bags is revealed and laid out on a large wooden table covered with a waxed tablecloth with a flower pattern: it is a hundred vacuum packages, all the same size, and the weight of ten grams each, with the name of the variety marked on it. I watch the scene as a silent spectator, I mind my own business and I keep my head down avoiding crossing glances. Entering the house, in the corner of my eye, I spot a gun leaning on the glass coffee table in front of a person not too reassuring, with tattoos all over his face, with whom I prefer not to become acquainted. My friend takes some packs of ganja, shakes some hands, hugs the guy with the suitcase, and we go back to where we came from.

I enter the car and start admonishing my contact, telling him not to involve me anymore in such affairs. My job now is running a magazine where cannabis is its main topic. It would not be very smart to be pinched in similar situations, where explaining your non-involvement would not exactly be a picnic.

I return to Milan and we send the latest issue of *Dolce Vita* to press, with two big pieces of news: the number of pages has gone from forty-eight to sixty, and on the cover there is the price of one euro. From today, our bimonthly magazine will no longer be free, but will have this symbolic cost that, above all will, allow us to track the distribution and avoid unnecessary waste.

The free-press are a cunning system of editors and advertisers that sell spaces to companies and avoid having to deal with the public. Whether readers like it or not, a free-press in fact gets printed and distributed anyway, as long as the game holds.

Quality information is paid for. And that's what we want to do.

September 15, 2006: Oriana Fallaci dies.

> *Oriana Fallaci died last night. Great journalist and writer. I do not share – and hopefully I never will – her bellicose ideas, her aggressiveness, her "rage" and her "pride". Nevertheless, I recognize her greatness and her*

intelligence. I find it inexcusable, however, that a person like her, with the media power she had, was saying, or rather spurring, her readers to the "fight". I find it an irresponsible and dangerous thing. Anyway I hope for her that, at least now, she'll rest in peace.

Time flies and *Dolce Vita* grows. On the November issue we put our friend J-Ax on the cover with his first solo album, *Di sana Pianta*. In addition to being on the same topic as the magazine, I am convinced that he deserves it and I am glad to be able to support him – in my small way – in his new adventure.

In the same issue, Ivan Artucovich, a very good illustrator of Swiss origin and our collaborator from the beginning, gives us a cartoon that will remain in the history of *Dolce Vita* and therefore deserves a special quote. The drawing shows a corner of the Italian parliament and three politicians intent on satisfying their vices, cocaine, alcohol and sex. In front of them, a man showing his back, dressed in a white tunic, beard and long blond hair, holding a rock in his raised right hand and with his left indicating a tiny Hemp plant next to him. The writing in the foreground is brilliant and emblematic: "Congressmen! he who is without sin cast the first stone at her". A perfect insight into the depressing Italian political situation and the hypocritical prohibition put in place towards our favorite plant.

It's a good time for me. Everything is going fine, and the work starts to give me the satisfaction I was hoping for. I don't give an inch; I give my best and my days end late at night. I go to the gym twice a week, I go out few nights, and I spend the rest of the time on the computer, buried in books and on the phone. Saturday and Sunday make no difference to me from weekdays. I always work because basically it seems to me like I never work. I do what I love to do, so I perceive my investment of energy and time like everything but sacrifice. I feel well, creative, entrepreneurial and with the wind at my back.

I fly to Amsterdam with a collaborator of mine to meet new potential established sponsors and partners. We so end up visiting the main cannabis seedbank, those that collect and study the genetic varieties of the plant, such as the historical Sensi Seeds, Paradise Seeds, where Luc welcomes us, and the Green House Seed Co, where Arjan and Franco are waiting for us.

Finally, I'm going on to meet with the owner of a famous coffee-shop of the Dutch capital to discuss an advertising campaign in *Dolce Vita*. In his studio, on the top floor of one of these premises, he invites me to sit. The right wall of the room is a mosaic of monitors connected to a myriad of cameras that control every single space of the palace. The desk between us is almost empty, carrying only a few ordered white sheets of paper, a simple black biro pen and above all four money counting machines, which before this moment I have only seen in some banks. I ask myself the purpose of having four of those in the same place, side by side. One should be enough, I think, as you can already calculate a huge amount of money very quickly; with two you can double the speed. Having to use four of them, at the same time, means having to quickly count many, many coins.

He signs an annual advertising contract without too many questions and hands me a down payment. From that moment onward I will never see him again, nor will I receive news about him and his coffee-shops. He's basically going to lose his down payment, never sending us the graphics for the advertisements or responding to our emails.

I return to Italy and I have the confirmation that all my work is paying off. The meetings in Rome have been productive: from January, *Dolce Vita* will also be on newsstands. Not in all of them – there are too many – but at least in the main Italian cities.

The quote is true: you reap what you sow.

Chapter 10

WHAT ABOUT IN ITALY?

If in the United States the 1800s had been the century of the chase of cotton on Hemp and the 1900s the century of prohibition, what happened in Italy in the meantime? Did anybody sow and harvest Hemp?

In reality in Italy, as seen elsewhere, the Hemp story had begun much earlier.

It was the Roman legions who introduced her cultivation in Italy in the first century C.E. in order to make ropes and sails for warships. Hemp is already mentioned in the *De Rustica* by Columella and in the *Naturalis Historia* by Pliny the Elder. Throughout all classical antiquity this remained her main application, until the first centuries of the Middle Ages, when Hemp became predominant in the countryside of much of the country.

At the rise of the Age of Commons, around the 11th century, the Po valley was literally invaded by her. The Venetian merchant industry required large quantities of Hemp and in Bologna and Ferrara the collection and processing of the fiber was organized to be exported to the marine power. In the countryside, the reclamation of the swampy terrains took place in order to be able to increase production.

Peasant families soon learned to take advantage of her infinite resources and so boosted their poor domestic economies of the time, making threads and ropes to weave clothes and sheets, using the seeds for soups or as cheap and nutritious feed for the birds, which also made them sing more, hence proving useful for the hunting season.

In 1617, the Piedmontese government invested in the construction of the first modern Hemp rope factory, a work considered strategic for supplying the Savoy army, while the port of Genoa became the export hub from which the increasingly valuable and requested Italian Hemp sailed to be delivered to many European countries, starting with neighboring France.

Throughout the whole eighteenth century, as we have already seen in France and England, also in the Bel Paese, the cultivation of Hemp expanded and stimulated the development of the technical innovations of the first industrial revolution. The cultivation of this Plant was so important throughout Italy to shape the landscape, the topography and more generally the social and urban organization.

In 1820, the Bourbon government finished the construction of what in fact it was the first highway in Naples. Over twenty kilometers of road crossed the Flegree hills to join the fields north of the Campanian capital with Lake Agnano. The road, now known as the Milan-Agnano, was called "Hemp road". Its purpose was in fact to facilitate the transport of one of the main resources of the kingdom, Hemp indeed, starting from the green areas of Secondigliano, where it was produced, up to the great lake where the process of maceration of the stems was carried out.

Thinking about it today may surprise many, but for centuries in the provinces of Naples and Caserta the presence of Hemp was impressive. The countryside in which it was being cultivated were organized as independent production centers, situated around the farmhouses, i.e. settlements of more groups of families dedicated to Hemp culture who, over time, became real municipalities. Secondigliano, Vomero, Posillipo, Capodimonte, Antignano, Arenella and many other villages, now bigger and densely inhabited, were born exactly like this.

The imprint of the unmistakable plant has left indelible marks in many other areas of Italy, from North to South, with a presence still evident and perceptible today. It is not uncommon to find places that have taken their names precisely from the traditional Hemp crop, such as Canevoi in Belluno or the entire region of Canavese in Piedmont. Some cities were so shaped by the history of Hemp to the point of inserting the drawing of her stem in their banner, as in the case of St. Mark the Evangelist in Campania. That's without even counting the urban centers that have dedicated a street or a square to her: Hemp Street in Bologna, Ferrara and dozens of other cities; Little Hemp Street in Cesena, Big Hemp Street in Forlì, Hemp Production Street in Udine, Hempy Street in Rome and Cagliari... and I could go on for a couple of pages without being able to mention them all.

What about in Italy?

In Bologna even today, walking under the arcades of the central Indipendenza street, you can admire the ancient fresco on which the writings *Panis vita, Canabis Protectio, Vinum laetitia*[57] stand out on the top of a woman intent on working the Hemp stems on the loom.

All these are indelible signs of a past that is impossible to erase, even though little is told.

In 1870, the Savoy army entered Rome and completed the unification of the peninsula. Immediately the newborn Italian State took care of the rationalization of Hemp national production in order to strengthen the country's economy. One of the first initiatives was the foundation in Milan of the first national flax and Hemp mill, an innovative center which spins and transforms Hemp and flax, coming from all over Italy, into products for export and consumption.

In the following decades, factories of this type keep on increasing, providing employment for about twenty thousand people who produced yarns for weaving, carpets, curtains, slits and ropes, sails and sacks, yarn for sewing soles and for fishing, ropes for the marinas and for scaffolding, for cranes and hoists, supplies for the navy, army, railways, post offices and hospitals. A multitude of families supported by the economy of Hemp, to which the other tens of thousands that produced it in the fields were to be added.

The industrial plants were about twenty, distributed mainly in the North. The most modern of all was that of Lodi, built in 1906 and equipped with state-of-the-art machinery imported from England. All factories were close to a course of water, which served both for the production of steam energy necessary to operate the plants and for the processing of the spun. The workers, mainly women, worked on shifts to ensure a continuous cycle.

With this set up, Italy become the second largest producer of Hemp in the world by quantity, second only to Russia, and the most renowned in terms of quality. Half of the harvest was destined for export

---

[57] From the Latin: "Bread is life, Cannabis is protection, wine is joy".

throughout Europe, where Italian Hemp was highly requested for her fiber that was both soft and incredibly durable.

During the First World War, however, all Hemp national production was put at the service of the Government, and in 1918, the trade union for Hemp spinners and weavers was registered at the Ministry of Industry. In addition, many factories had to increase production, because the import of flax was suddenly halted.

With the coming to power of fascism the situation did not change. Benito Mussolini in 1925 stated:

> *Hemp has been put on the agenda of the nation by the Duce, because par autarkic excellence it is destined to emancipate us as much as possible from the burdensome toll that we still have towards other countries in the textile fibers sector. It's not just the agricultural economic side, there's also the social side whose incidence could not be better highlighted than from the following figure: thirty thousand workers to whom the Italian Hemp industry gives work*[58].

Fascism also founded the National Hemp Consortium and in 1933 constituted the Mandatory Provincial Consortia required for the defense of Hemp cultivation, i.e. provincial corporate bodies entrusted with the direction and implementation of the plant's economy in all territories. Aided also by the beginning of the expansion of war campaigns, which demanded a great effort on Italian agriculture to compensate for the collapse of the imports, in the five-year period between 1936 and 1940, the production of Hemp in Italy marked its historical record, surpassing for the first time one hundred thousand tons.

But it was her swan song.

So, as we have seen for the United States, also in Italy the joint assault of cheaper cotton, synthetic fibers and prohibition succeeded, in a few years, in tearing to pieces one of the longest-lived and most important production sectors of the peninsula.

---

[58] Cristina Bregoli, *History of industrial Hemp in Italy from 1873 to 1923*, Soft Secret No. 1, 2004.

What about in Italy?

Until siding with Nazi Germany, relations between the Italian and the United States governments were cordial and Mussolini often went to pay visits to the overseas power to get respect in front of the Star and Stripes nation. For this reason, it is not surprising that in the 1930s, the fascist regime was among the first to take onboard the call for war against "marijuana", renamed by the duce as the "nigger drug".

In Italy, the use of cannabis as a drug was practically unknown, and there were not even the circles of jazz music, or cinema artists that had spread its first consumption in the United States. At most, the dried flowers of plants grown for textile purposes, with very low-to-no psychoactive property, were smoked by farmers to make up for the misery that prevented the purchase of more expensive tobacco. Despite this, Hemp was included in the list of "poisonous substances having a narcotic action" regulated by the Penal Code of 1930. Article 447 of the Code punished the sale and facilitation of the consumption of any prohibited substance, while Article 729 punishes with a prison sentence or fine those who "are caught in a state of severe psychic alteration for the abuse of narcotic substance in a public place". Personal consumption remained excluded from the criminal circuit, but it wasn't good news. For fascism, in fact, drug use was to be considered a severe pathology, to be taken care of with a mandatory stay at mental illness facilities. Whoever was caught smoking a joint would have ended up in a psychiatric hospital.

In the post-war period the situation did not change until 1954, when the Italian government largely copied the drug legislation approved in the United States by President Truman just three years earlier. The new law envisaged prison for anyone who "buys, sells, exports, imports substances or mixed listed in the list of drugs". Criminal prohibition then made its entry into Italian legislation, a few years before the UN Convention which in 1961 made it mandatory for each nation.

For the Italian Hemp farmer, life got tougher and tougher. In the North, the farmers found jobs in factories and Hemp production was quickly abandoned everywhere, except for a small area around Ferrara, while in the South it went on – if only for a lack of alternatives – but amid a thousand difficulties. No national business plan seemed to want to deal with reviving a crop which, in order to stay competitive with synthetic fibers from the United States and from England, needed investment. The National Hemp Consortium, left to ruins, had no means for providing the modernization of production or to mechanize the various stages of processing, making it faster and cheaper. They kept on using outdated techniques, the same handed down from generation to generation for centuries: water maceration, crushing of the stems, kneading with heavy and anachronistic wooden tools, and hand binding of stacks.

But out there the world was running fast, and in this way it couldn't work. In the countryside of Caserta, the peasants made themselves heard and the government pretended to take ownership of the problem. In 1951, a major conference for the revival of Hemp farming was organized in Frattamaggiore (Naples) in which several MPs participated. The same happened in Ferrara in January 1955. But they were all initiatives with the only objective of stemming the protests, without being then followed by any actual measures.

In December 1975, the government, led by the Christian Democrat Aldo Moro, passed a new drug law in which the distinction between consumption and sales reappeared, and only the latter was punished with prison. A small improvement for consumers who, especially among the younger generations, began to increase in numbers in Italy, but no improvement for Hemp farming. More and more police officers, searching for self-production practices of marijuana run by young hippies, seized and sealed even the cultivation of industrial Hemp. The few agricultural entrepreneurs who still cultivated the plant, among countless economic issues, risked finding themselves embroiled in judicial trials.

It was way too much.

In 1978, the last fields dedicated to Hemp farming were abandoned. In just thirty years Italy had sacrificed, through the war on cannabis, a vital economic sector, that gave work to tens of thousands of families.

In the definition adopted by the UN Convention, prohibition should have "freed the world from drugs." The Italian case is perfect to understand how the only thing it managed to eradicate was instead the green and sustainable Hemp industry, while the consumption of cannabis, like any other type of banned substance, did nothing but grow out of proportion.

The 1980s were years of political disengagement. Millions of Italians were hypnotized by the entertainment and the undressed girls seizing the screens of the new private TVs of Silvio Berlusconi. In the meantime, on the streets, crowds of kids were abusing heroin, which was claiming over five hundred lives per year by overdose. And hundreds more, which quickly became thousands, were infected with AIDS through unprotected sex and the exchange of infected syringes. Newspapers, as always, in search of easy catchy slogans, were speaking of a "lost generation".

Cannabis, on the other hand, kept on claiming no lives, but its criminalization only increased. Politicians, therapists, columnists, editorials, priests and know-it-alls, were overcrowding newspapers and TVs to express, with different turns of phrase, always the same mantra: "Drug addicts die from heroin but they start with joints, so to solve the plague of drugs we have to first tackle the consumption of marijuana".

It was the "passing theory". From a scientific point of view, it was a total hoax, unmasked already at the time of the "La Guardia report", but it is still spread today, with no punishment.

In those years, the United States President was Ronald Reagan, former Hollywood actor, who was advocating an economy of unrestrained liberalism and the repression approach for managing every form of what he considered social deviance. What was supposed to be a war on drugs soon became a war on drug addicts, with millions of consumers jailed for possession of modest amounts of any type of illegal substance.

The doctrine of "zero tolerance" also conquered the head of the Italian government Bettino Craxi, at the time, a rising star of politics and eager to credit himself as a resolute and innovative statesman in front of the voters. The media simplification that he chose to use to impose his own recipe against the drug emergency was a syllogism of granted effect: if it is forbidden to sell, it must be prohibited even to buy.

After long parliamentary discussions the law advocated by Craxi became state law in November 1990[59]. The law made the distinction between "soft" and "heavy" drugs, but it contemplated detention even for personal consumption for both categories. The effects of these tougher restrictions did not take long to present the bill. The detainees doubled in a short time: from 25,804 inmates present in the penitentiaries at the end of 1990 to more than fifty thousand units in just three years. Drug addicts doubled from seven thousand to almost fifteen thousand and a third of them ended up in jail[60].

The disastrous Craxi recipe, however, generated an unexpected twist. An anti-prohibitionist movement took hold in Italy demonstrating – against all expectations – that it was well-rooted among citizens, evidently not convinced of the reasons for prohibition despite decades of biased propaganda. Many associations launched the proposal for a referendum against criminal sanctions for consumers. The idea was first bashfully collected by the now moribund Communist Party and then, with much more enthusiasm, from the radicals of Marco Pannella, who launched himself in the referendum campaign with the usual acts of civil disobedience, even going so far as to suffer a trial for freely distributing hashish in the squares. In a few months, the necessary signatures were collected and on 18 April 1993, over nineteen million voters buried the Craxi reform, establishing that the use of cannabis and any other substance should not be considered a crime[61].

In those days Italy was politically on the brink of collapse, a situation that for many citizens was in truth a new hope. For months the ruling class trembled under the blows of the "Clean Hands" pool. A group of Milanese judges, led by magistrate Antonio Di Pietro, was in fact investigating the corruption that for years had affected all main parties.

---

[59] The law is classified as DPR 309/90, but was immediately renamed "Iervolino-Vassalli", after the name of the two members of parliament who signed the proposal, Rosa Russo Iervolino (Republican) and Giuliano Vassalli (Democrat).

[60] F. Corleone, A. Magara, D*rug war: collateral damage*, Edizioni Polistampa, 2010.

[61] A total of 36,911,398 voters went to the polls. The votes in favor of the referendum were 19,255,915, 55.36% of the total valid votes.

What about in Italy?

Tangentopoli: this is how the scandal that implicated all the leading players in Italian politics was renamed.

Bettino Craxi was under pressure more than anyone else; many investigations concerned him personally, and within a few weeks he received as many as eleven warrants. He resigned from the position of Prime Minister, but the parliamentarian's colleagues spared him from arrest. On 29 April 1993, the Chamber of Deputies denied the Judiciary the permission to proceed against him, recurring to the parliamentary immunity clause. The following day, two weeks after the referendum, he was in a room at the Raphael Hotel, in the center of Rome, when he began to hear a strange noise coming from the square below, a buzzing that began to grow and quickly became a mass protest. Hundreds of people were barely kept at a safe distance from the front door by police, when someone had begun waving a note of ten thousand lire (roughly today US$10); soon everyone copied the gesture, and a chorus rose: "Take these ones too, Bettino, take these ones too!" Craxi faced the situation with style – it must be admitted – refusing to retreat via the exit at the back of the building, and walking through the people in the square, with his head up high, jumping in the car while the coins thrown by the crowd rained down on him.

It was the end of a forty-year era. No more Christian Democracy and Socialist Party, while the Communists changed their names. It was all downhill for Silvio Berlusconi who simply filled his TV with infinite election promises, and then succeeded to become Prime Minister the following year.

The cannabis battle continued. After the referendum victory, the anti-prohibitionists launched a new challenge: collecting the five hundred thousand signatures necessary to propose a referendum for removing cannabis from the list of prohibited substances, and therefore its legalization. In 1995, the stands for collecting signatures throughout Italy were put in place. It took only a few months to gather more than half a million names, and in January 1996 the referendum proposal was officially filed. Nevertheless, the Italian citizens were not allowed to express themselves, as the Constitutional Court did not approve of the referendum proposal on the grounds that it would go against a law that was bound by international treaties signed by Italy, i.e. the UN Convention on Drugs of 1961.

The Second Republic was unfolding, and for many aspects it did not seem so different from the First one. It certainly wasn't on the approach to Hemp.

In 2001, Berlusconi returned to government leading a coalition which included Umberto Bossi's Northern League, the post fascist of National Alliance, and survivors of the *Christian Democracy* diaspora, who merged into the *Union of The Centre* led by Pier Ferdinando Casini, among which was a character who will be part of the story of Hemp for many more years to come: Carlo Giovanardi.

AN leader Gianfranco Fini immediately announced that among his goals was to pass a new law on drugs even more repressive than Craxi's. He too started his battle creating a slogan that would lead the way to the re-equation between light and heavy drugs: "Drugs are drugs." Toxicologists, researchers and the bulk of halfway houses emphasized the non-sense of the statement, but Fini – adamant – introduced his bill. His party also realized a commercial to push parliament to act; however time was passing, and the proposal continued to be on hold at the Commission of Justice. We then arrived at the summer of 2005 and the end of the legislature, scheduled for the following spring, loomed making sure that nothing would have happened.

It was at this point that, in aid of the former Deputy Prime Minister came Carlo Giovanardi, just appointed referent of the Department of Anti-drug policies from the Berlusconi government. His idea was cunning. There was no more time to make a new law on drugs; so it was better to make changes to the existing one and try to insert it in a decree to shorten the time, making its approval possible.

The good opportunity came the following January, while the government was preparing a maxi-decree for the Winter Olympics that a few weeks later would be held in Turin. The two decided to try and, between the articles that talked about the fight against doping between athletes, they inserted the changes to the drug legislation. One of the usual political tricks of our ruling class. Obstruction from the opposition was not enough: the decree passed with 271 yes votes and 190 no votes.

What about in Italy?

From the seats of the National Alliance party a long applause arose. With only two months left to the end of the legislature, the prohibitionist dream became a reality. "Drugs are drugs."

By law, possessing marijuana or heroin was the same thing and the punishment ranged from six to twenty years in prison. Even the effects of the referendum that had decriminalized consumption were eased, moving to target the purchase and consumption in groups thanks to the ingenious insertion of a new word in the text: "exclusively". If before "personal consumption" was allowed, now, with the definition of "exclusively personal consumption", those who bought weed for themselves and a couple of friends became drug dealers.

It was a full-fledged infamous law, a sword of Damocles above the head of every cannabis consumer, a tool of obvious relentlessness towards citizens who hurt no one, and they only demanded that their personal freedoms be respected.

The Fini-Giovanardi law, this was how the legislation was then called (law 49/2006), managed in a few years to break every record in Republican history. With only one article, it produced 38.5% of Italian prison inmates. Over twenty-six thousand people ended up in prison for violating the norm and most of them were made up of consumers or small cannabis dealers found with a few grams.

The law, moreover, succeeded in giving the final coup de grace to a judicial system already congested, and certainly not renowned for its speed, loading it with over two hundred and twenty thousand criminal trials. Thousands more consumers, then, found themselves dealing with absurd administrative penalties: driving licenses suspended for smoking a joint even several days before driving, mandatory rehabilitation courses, dismissals, expatriation bans and the withdrawal of passports.

In the meantime, Carlo Giovanardi's twin brother, Daniele, was president of the Brotherhood of Mercy, a charity giant that, among other things, ran recovery centers for drug addicts. A nice conflict of interest in the family, in short, but that couldn't really worsen the sad picture of the history of the cannabis in Italy of those years.

The witch hunt had begun also on our peninsula and the Great Inquisitor was Carlo Giovanardi.

Chapter 11

COUNTERINFORMATION AND TRUTH

To counter the icy inquisitorial climate brought by the Fini-Giovanardi law – the infamous law representing a sword of Damocles above the head of every cannabis consumer – it would take a compact and well-organized anti-prohibitionist movement to awaken public opinion and warm the consciences. Unfortunately, in 2006, in Italy it was not present.

Thus, when the law was passed, the reaction is weak and the only noteworthy action is the attempt to bring together all active realities in a project called "ConFini Zero" whose slogan is: "Right or wrong, it can't be a crime". Some initiatives are reasonably successful, but nothing could really undermine the institutional position and change the mind of the Government. There is no reason for explaining such relentlessness towards people who don't hurt anyone and just ask that their personal freedoms are respected.

On *Dolce Vita* we give voice and space to those who fight against this repression, activists, associations and meeting organizers. The magazine becomes an important channel for all of them and a lone voice between the aligned and homogenized panorama of the national media.

In the January 2007 issue, for the first time we publish an article on climate change, leaving a serious and unequivocal warning. We talk about the Gulf Stream, floods, drought, but above all of future scenarios with mass migrations and geographical redistribution of the population. In hindsight, we got it right or maybe – unlike others – we had the courage to address the issue without filters.

The group of collaborators continues to grow. It is our priority to take care of the quality of the content and the new entry of this period is Jorge Cervantes, an international expert in the cultivation of cannabis and author of one of the most famous and sold books ever written on the art of self-production, that is, The Marijuana Bible. On our pages he inaugurates his column entitled Cervantes School, with articles that are real gospel truth, especially for novice growers.

At the same time, we participate as exhibitors in the most important European fairs of the sector, from Madrid to London, and Basel to Barcelona, we start to become the Italian point of reference for Hemp culture. New companies invest in the magazine purchasing advertising space and this gives us the opportunity to continue to grow, step by step. We debate complex topics, like the shootings in American schools related to the abuse of psychiatric drugs, and others much lighter, but never examined in depth by the media, such as rave culture and *teknotribes*. I'm more and more proud of what *Dolce Vita* is becoming!

Spring flies away, summer too, and I don't even take a break. Ghosts are part of my past and I'm fine now, but I keep fighting with the world: sometimes I feel a complete misfit, at other times I have a great guilty feeling by perfectly fitting in this society and its rotten system. And I reflect it in my diary:

> *I'm not sure about you, but personally I'm struggling more and more to understand this world. It's upside down. It's weird. It's wrong.*
>
> *I try daily to enjoy it, I really put all my effort in trying to find the bright side of things, to convince me that sooner or later everything will change. And at the end of the day, I have to say that I'm doing pretty well: I often have fun, many times I fall asleep peacefully and wake up full of good intentions, and it doesn't take me much to grasp and appreciate all the positivity that surrounds me.*
>
> *Other times, however, I sink into such an abyss of uncertainties and perplexity that I come out distressed, troubled, and despaired - that I feel leaves heavy consequences. I question everything, I wonder where we're going, what we're doing, why.*

I help a friend open the first grow shop in the province of Belluno. It's called Boomalek, it's in Feltre and it's not a simple shop, but an anti-prohibitionist stronghold in an area of Italy where cannabis is still particularly disputed and demonized.

Then Scott Blakey Shantibaba invites me to Campione and there, along with him and Filimagno, another dear friend of mine, "Cannapioneer" and fore runner of biological fertilizers, I spend a day to be remembered, between the lake and a joint of hashish from 1998, of a quality that you cannot understand.

But the time had come to be on the move again, to start discovering the world, as my parents taught me as a child. And so I leave for a trip on the road in Portugal and Spain, together with a childhood friend. Lisbon, Faro, Seville, Cordoba, Granada, Malaga: new stimuli, new oxygen, inputs and inspirations.

On my return, it's time to close issue number twelve of October 2007. The logo of *V for Vendetta* stands on the new cover and, on the inside, on two pages as heavy as wood, we publish the complete and detailed list of the Italian Parliamentarians with criminal records. The only national and legally registered magazine to do so.

In Bologna, and in two hundred other Italian squares, on 8 September, the first V-Day organized by Beppe Grillo takes place, during which three hundred thousand signatures are collected for the proposal of a law of popular initiative. We're on the ball!

That day *Dolce Vita* somehow gets to the Genoese comedian just as he speaks on stage, and he holds it in his hand for the entire duration of the main speech. The following day some of the most popular national newspapers publish the picture of Grillo with this strange and unknown magazine under his arm. I am forced to disprove rumors of any kind, conspiracies, secret alliances and so on and so forth.

I keep working hard, ending my days at four or five in the morning and starting the next ones just few hours after.

Our friend J-Ax suggests we interview a new artist of Sicilian origins that - he assures - will soon become one of the kings of Italian rap. His name is Marracash and J-Ax was not wrong. I meet him right in the home of the former Article 31 member and I pack up a good interview that we then publish in issue thirteen of *Dolce Vita*. We are among the very first magazines to talk about him. "Marra" is just at the beginning of his career and will soon take flight with singles on the radio and contracts with the majors.

Hemp, an incredible story

It's winter. Milan saddens me, I'm uncomfortable with too many people, the chaos on public transport, air pollution. So, I come back more and more often to my small mountain village in the Belluno Dolomites.

December 2007. I launch a new online forum along the lines of *Enjoint* but exclusively dedicated to the cultivation of cannabis. It's called *Overgrow.it* and it's along the lines of the American version, a point of global reference for all growers. I will manage it for a year, and after that I will give it away to re-devote myself to *Enjoint* with more dedication, avoiding dispersing forces and resources.

In the same period, we go out with the first issue of *Dolce Vita Urban*, i.e. a free and reduced edition, printed and distributed in fifty thousand copies. The project includes a first winter issue and a second one in summer for a total of one hundred and fifty thousand copies to promote *Dolce Vita* and introduce it to new readers. No one ever in Italy has published a magazine dedicated to cannabis in such big numbers.

Into the Wild comes out in cinemas, a stunning movie by Sean Penn from Jon Krakauer's book that tells the story – a true story – of a fearless traveler, lonely and unlucky. It will soon become the manifesto of a new generation of travelers, myself included.

A few months later the first iPhone arrives on the market. We talk about it too in the new column Hi-tech because it's a revolution in the world of communication.

I start being recognized as a journalist in the region of Lombardy thanks to the work with *Dolce Vita* and the many articles produced. Not that I needed it, but it's more of a small personal and symbolic revenge towards the university that wanted me to make copies in some anonymous publishing company.

A book appears on the shelves of Italian bookshops that shortly becomes an editorial case. It is Gomorrah by Saviano, and everyone talks about it.

2007 is gone.

I take advantage of my column in issue fourteen dated January 2008 to clarify some aspects of my work and activity.

Counterinformation and truth

It often happens that when I meet new people, they ask me what I do, what is my job and my commitments. Those who are satisfied with the traditional answer that "I do a little bit of everything" are fine with that; those more curious or who want to deepen my knowledge struggle to understand. Because the "problem" is that I really do a little bit of everything and this seems impossible to them.

I'm now 24 years old, and it's true that I'm a particular guy, entrepreneurial, active, full of energy (as all my peers should be), of ideas, fantasy and desire to do, but it is also true that we live in an era and in a place where if you want to live, and not simply exist, you have to roll up your sleeves,, no matter what. With or without imagination.

I admit I was lucky, since my family provided for me in my youth, but anyone who is now reading these lines had the same luck compared to most of the world's population, those who truly live in the third world where drinking a glass of clean water is not a given.

Then there is no excuse for anyone; and what I've got has always been earned. So, if anyone was thinking of accusing me of being daddy's boy cliché, I'm here to say that this is simply not true.

That said, this is not intended to be a self-celebration: to put it briefly, I am mainly involved in communication, I have my own company, I manage about ten websites, different publications (including Dolce Vita), but I'm also involved in some commercial, artistic, cultural and leisure activities, and in my free time - I travel.

I'm not an alien, it's the people around me who increasingly make me feel that way.

There's such an apathy around that it's astonishing. My generation is still, motionless, looks at the world while it's spinning (poorly) without moving a finger. Anything that scares it, it always feels too immature, too fragile, powerless.

> *My parents' generation, on the other hand, is tired, it has already given what it had, and then, as you know, at a certain age now it's not easy to get back into the game. But I don't care much about them, I mean... I hope that they enjoyed it, but I can't do much else.*
>
> *This thought is instead for those who are still in their "prime time", like me: wake up!*
>
> *Look around you, be curious all the time, read, get informed, watch movies or go to the theater, browse on the internet, travel if you can, engage in something you believe in, believe in something, look for something to believe in, and to commit yourself to, do not settle, never, do not let yourself down, never, never stop, never. Get passionate, fall in love, with yourself, with life, with the world...*

The more I have the opportunity to inform myself independently, to scrutinize, to study the news and the facts, the more I realize how crooked this world is. And I find it hard to find serenity, seeing around me too much resignation. More and more often, the guilty are not punished and it is, as always, the good people who suffer. The politics is rotten, especially in Italy. Law enforcement, instead of enforcing the rules, often break them. The information is fake, filtered, piloted. The whole system is focused on consumption and material goods.

I write in my diary fighting and indignant words:

> *The Prodi government is over. Mastella's resignation sent it into crisis. In parliament some members of the Northern League celebrated popping bottles of prosecco and eating mortadella. There was also a brawl, some spitting and someone feeling unwell. The Campania region is inundated with garbage. There are strikes everywhere. One in three families struggles to make it to the end of the month. Politicians take tens of thousands of Euros in salaries, golden pensions, they don't pay taxes, they don't pay houses, they don't pay for transportation. They simply don't pay.*

Counterinformation and truth

> *On TV they show us the usual four pricks who make the conga line on Sundays or win fake money in some more and more silly quiz. I've had enough. People have had enough. But nothing happens. Nothing ever happens. How is it possible that nothing ever happens?! We need a revolution. Peaceful or not! At this point there is no other solution. People have to get their lives back, fuck!*

In Cannabusiness, however, a revolution happens, and it is that of the auto-flowering seeds, that is those that give plants that can automatically bloom regardless of the number of daylight hours received each day. As a rule of thumb, cannabis plants require eighteen hours of light and six of dark in the vegetative phase and, subsequently, in the blooming phase, twelve hours of light and twelve hours of darkness. Auto-flowering plants are a novelty that speeds up and simplifies the cultivation process and thus getting new growers interested to the self-production of cannabis.

I am contacted by a Slovenian boy named Matej who proposes to create a version of *Dolce Vita* for the Balkans. The year before, we had attempted to launch *Dolce Vita International*, i.e. the English version of the magazine, to be distributed throughout Europe through trade fairs. The initiative had started well, but despite all I decided to interrupt it after two issues for too many logistical problems and the risk of not being able to guarantee to sponsors an excellent service. But now Matej assures me that he would take care of 100% of the new project without burdening our staff. I follow my instinct and decide to trust him, I give him the okay and so *Dolce Vita Slovenia* is born, which shortly afterwards will become *Dolce Vita Balkan*, in two languages – Slovenian and Croatian – which is also distributed in Serbia and Montenegro: the first magazine on the topic ever published in the Balkans.

Social networks arrive, MySpace is a hit, and it seems is suddenly upstaging all the other sites. It's great innovation, because it's the users themselves that create the content, the network, to connect between each other, among a like and a comment.

With *Dolce Vita* so far, we've always focused much on the paper version, also because *Enjoint* has always been our online reference point. But now with the newborn MySpace channel we reach thousands of new readers interested in publishing and in the content we produce. The magazine grows by leaps and bounds.

Albert Hofmann, the already mentioned father of LSD, dies on 28 April 2008 at the age of one hundred and two.

In Milan, I have the pleasure of meeting Fritz da Cat, the historic DJ of the old hip hop school and now international entrepreneur of spray cans for writers. We have a few business lunches and dinners, speculating on possible collaborations and extravagant revolutionary projects that will never come to life.

On 31 May, at the Kindergarten in Bologna Delirium is staged, a mega party organized by *Dolce Vita*, in conjunction with the fourth – and last– iteration of *Cannabis Strong Type*. On stage Boom Draw Int., Inoki, Marracash and Vincenzo Da Via Anfossi, deejay Nymph and other artists alternate. In addition to live music, we organize a live painting show with Raptuz and Gatto, international renowned writers, and a burlesque show by the Sick Girl.

It's a great night for *Dolce Vita*.

And it's the beginning of a great summer for me. I turn twenty-five and I feel on fire.

I write between my notes:

> *I am traveling with some friends, our destinations are Barcelona, Valencia, Zaragoza. After this adventure, in a couple of weeks, I will leave for the States.*
>
> *I'm trying to combine my passion for travel with work.*
>
> *I feel more and more the need to move, to travel, to discover. I feel more and more the need to go. And the more I see, the more I discover, the more I go... the more I feel the need to do it again. Every new road I walk is different from any other road I've taken before, and every city I visit has a different sky from any other. Different scents, different colors, different sounds and noises. This infinite originality pushes me to look for more, and more, and more.*

Counterinformation and truth

Given this attitude of mine stopping in one place, with all the comforts that this implies, and put down imaginary roots fueled by routing would be an injustice to myself. Injustice that once old, I'm sure of this, I wouldn't ever forgive myself for. I have therefore decided that, at this moment in my life, I will devote all my energies to traveling, traveling and traveling again!

Traveling makes me feel more alive than anything else in the world.

Traveling makes me feel, more than anything else, part of the world.

During the Spanish trip, I smoke few joints after years of sobriety. My head is clear from any paranoia, I am serene, and in fact I feel great, and I much enjoy it. Cannabis enhances our moods, for better or for worse. It's important to always keep this in mind and be aware of it to be able to know how to manage the signals that you can get by smoking it.

I decide to add substance to the contents of *Dolce Vita* and to increase the number of pages dedicated to counter-information, investigative journalism and to thorny subjects. I thus engage Antonino Monteleone, a young intrepid journalist born in Reggio Calabria who writes about political and judicial news. In the new issue we inaugurate a column entitled *Radio London*, inspired by radio programs broadcasted during the fascist regime by English radio BBC. I'll leave him carte blanche and ask him to offer us articles without filters, without mincing words, articles that no one else in Italy would dare to publish.

And then I throw myself into traveling, making it become a new project: I find sponsors and partners willing to support my new American trip in exchange of visibility and promotion. A coast to coast ten thousand kilometers long, from New York to San Francisco, detouring to Canada. I open a dedicated blog, I sign collaborations for local newspapers and radios, I print stickers to customize the car that I will be using during the trip and leave for one and a half months of vacation at no cost. Basically, I improvise myself as travel blogger and influencer a few years ahead of time.

It turned out to be a month and a half working double time, between managing remotely *Dolce Vita*, feeding the new blog dedicated to travel, following the radios and newspapers, but above all, to complying with the timetable. It's not by chance that I return eight kilos lighter, although American cuisine is certainly not the most light or healthy.

In the nineteenth issue of December 2008, we talk about the Mafia in Milan, in view of expo 2015, of *Notte della Taranta*, of hydroponics cultivation, ketamine, the glorious anti-fascist barricades of Parma, of a trip to Burgundy and the Bonobos as an evolution of the human species, of Luis Buñuel, of virtual reality, fetish, and finally we interview Dargen D'Amico and Alborosie!

But it's not all smooth sailing. As the magazine grows, so do the problems to be solved, as do the demands of some sponsors who, as advertisers, are convinced that they have the right to decide the contents and dictate the law. I stay firm and reject some plugs and automatically lose the financial support of a couple of companies, including that from one of the most important in the European sector. The immediate result is losing out in terms of revenue, but I know that in time we will be rewarded in terms of credibility.

Milan suffocates me, there is too much of everything. Too much for me. After five years spent there, I slowly decide to go back to where I came from, in my mountain village, and rent a studio where I can stay quiet and take refuge from time to time. The parties, the socialites, the thousand contacts that the city offers, don't make up for my need of contact with nature, of a slower life, of sobriety. This is the direction of my "*Dolce Vita*".

On 13 November 2008, under the initiative of a pitiful public prosecutor of Ferrara, the police trigger an absurd blitz totaling one hundred and fifty-six frisks of grow shops all over Italy, issuing sixty-two warrants for the crime of incitement to the unlawful use of drugs. In the months and years to come, all offenders will be acquitted, but the bureaucratic and legal consequences will cause the closure of several shops and companies.

The operation, under all circumstances, certainly had a big cost for taxpayers: the question is also raised by a senator through a parliamentary enquiry, which of course never received an answer.

I too was searched in my apartment in Milan: four plainclothes policemen ring the doorbell with particular eagerness at six in the morning. I open a few inches and the safety chain goes into tension. They initially push, believing they have green light, then they stop and tell me to unlock the chain. I tell them to calm down, not to make too much noise as it's early and they disturb the neighbors, but above all to show me the documents and the search warrant. Faced with calm and confidence they immediately change their attitude and settle down. I let them in and offer them coffee. Amazed at the gesture, they thank me without accepting. At that point the search becomes a mere due act, and they don't even delve through my things. They admit to knowing barely anything about the "cannabis issue" and the laws governing grow shops, but they have simply received orders from their superiors and have to execute them. They eventually seized some copies of *Dolce Vita*, some cannabis seeds and a chillum. All things that I show them out of my own free will and that they seal in a box with cord and lacquer wax. They leave it at my home begging me not to open it until there is an eventual seized order. We greet each other with courtesy; they too, in the end, perhaps realize of the absurdity of all this.

"There's probably no God! Now stop worrying and enjoy your life": these are the cubital letterings on the cover of issue number twenty of *Dolce Vita* coming out in February 2009. It is a phrase taken up and translated by the shock campaign of an English atheist association who recently caused havoc in the UK. But we are in Italy though, home of the Vatican and the Pope, so the provocation is even stronger. Many tell us we're crazy to do such a thing, at such a time, in such a nation. We know that, but we are neither crazy nor careless: we have a powerful means of communication available, and we feel we have the responsibility of using it to tell the truth, no matter what, even if doing it means taking risks.

In Italy, the socio-political situation is quite embarrassing. We are the laughing state of Europe, the Berlusconi government continues to collect gaffes and to enact shameful laws, limiting further the freedom of the press, suffocating any protest, increasing the privileges of the "caste". It seems like the country is about to go belly up at any moment.

New issue of *Dolce Vita*, new cover: the title reads Poor Italy and the shape of the nation contains a collage of the worst atrocities of the moment. In the background, the first articles of the constitution tipped over, upside down, like Italy.

On 15 April 2010, Jack Herer dies at the age of seventy, historic American activist, author of countless battles but especially of the aforementioned *The emperor wears no clothes*, the most famous and an important book that analyzes the prohibition of Hemp, that on *Dolce Vita* we started translating and episodically publishing for a few months. Thanks to him, since the first edition of 1985, millions of people became aware of the plot concocted against Hemp and of Hemp's countless uses.

In the meantime, Obama's United States has begun the spread of the "green revolution" and we go out with a headline on the subject of: *Yes we Can(nabis)*. The new US president legalizes therapeutic use in thirteen states and, indeed, opens the debate for a complete legalization of cannabis in the new continent. It is a historical moment, a turning point. Those same United States of America that eighty years before had begun the battle against our Beloved, imposing her prohibition to the rest of the world, today they are reassessing it.

Paradoxically, the reasons, as today as yesterday, are economical. Cash, money, bling-bling, dollars, Euros, dough, plata. Call them whatever you like, but it is what always rules the world, whether we like it or not. And as long as this will be the case – and I am increasingly convinced of this – there will never be peace for humanity.

Chapter 12

SHE HEALS

Although almost the entire history of the twentieth century has been marked by the fight against Hemp in the political field, scientists, universities and centers of research have – fortunately – never stopped studying her healing potential. And at the heart of the researchers' interest in recent decades has been a particular active ingredient present in thein the plant: cannabidiol (CBD), a molecule that does not generate psychoactive effects but possesses large and increasingly apparent medical properties.

CBD was first isolated by a team of researchers of the Department of Chemistry at the University of Illinois in 1940. But it still took some more time for Israeli doctor Raphael Mechoulam, now considered the father of cannabinoid research, to identify its exact structure, which he did in 1963.

Mechoulam was a mythical figure, a true pioneer of research. Had he achieved the same great results by studying some other plant or molecule there's no doubt that he would have received the most important awards in the scientific community. With *Dolce Vita* we had the privilege of being the only Italian newspaper to interview him, acquainting readers with a great man of science and – through its history – with a new chapter in the boycott of this magnificent plant.

For decades, in fact, his studies have been met with silence. In the early 1980s, for example, Dr. Mechoulam, together with his team, conducted the first research on the effect of cannabis in the treatment of refractory epilepsy, demonstrating how CBD was effective in the treatment of certain forms resistant to all drugs on the market. Yet that search did not interest anyone until a few years ago; at least now – with incredible delay – the truth of his study is coming out.

Fortunately for him, though now elderly, Dr. Mechoulam can finally take some nice revenge. And it was precisely the indomitable determination of extraordinary people like him that prevented everything from being lost and, despite the obscurantism imposed by politics, they made continuous strides forward possible.

Among them, one must be undoubtedly reference Rick Simpson, and Scott Blakey, better known as Shantibaba.

The former, a true forerunner of independent research, studied and developed by himself a cannabis oil for healing purposes. He first experimented on himself, after being struck by three melanomas; then he publicly committed to sharing the cure which, in his opinion, worked much better than any standard therapy. Opposed for years by pharmaceutical companies and official science, Simpson helped hundreds of sick people with his artisanal preparation since the early part of this millennium, when such a practice was still completely illegal in the United States.

On the other hand, Shantibaba is a true guru of cultivation and selection of varieties. First in the Netherlands and then in the United States with Mr. Nice Seedbank, he selected C=cannabis varieties focusing on the potential of different active ingredients. Thanks to his work today we have at our disposal species carefully designed for therapeutical use through the enhancement of CBD concentrations and balance with other active ingredients.

Having had him as editor of *Dolce Vita* from day one is a great privilege.

It is also thanks to these pioneers that, in recent years, research on cannabidiol was able to make giant steps. Regarding the treatment of refractory epilepsy, for example, Mechoulam's theories have been confirmed by dozens of studies. The most recent regarded sixty-six children affected by this pathology. The researchers from the Children's Hospital of the University Medical Centre of Ljubljana gave them eight milligrams a day of CBD, resulting in a decrease of at least 50% in convulsive attacks in 48.5% of cases and their total disappearance in

21.2%[62]. Thanks to this type of research, cannabis is today recognized as a drug against epilepsy in many nations.

Cannabis can also help to treat Alzheimer's. Its components in fact fight and help eliminate the toxic protein that causes this form of dementia. According to studies, cannabinoids can improve the lives of patients with this disease and act on brain receptors, both by preserving cognitive functions and by protecting the brain[63]. But that's not all. Cannabis is also useful in preventing the brain inflammation at the heart of the disease, preventing, or at least delaying, its onset[64].

There is also indisputable evidence in the treatment of another degenerative disease, Multiple Sclerosis (MS). In the prestigious scientific journal *Neurology*, a summary study was published which took into consideration all existing research on the effectiveness of cannabis related to the treatment of MS. The conclusions explain that she was unquestionably capable of mitigating symptoms of the pathology such as "spasticity symptoms, pain, and urinary frequency"[65]. For this treatment, a spray cannabis extract, to be orally taken, is already on the market. It's called Sativex and it's legally for sale in over thirty states, including Italy.

CBD – as well as THC – has proved effective in countering chronic and neuropathic pain in different pathologies. An example is the treatment of HIV-associated pain. After following sixteen HIV-positive patients, who reported benefits regarding perceived pain after smoking cannabis for a week, researchers from the University of San Francisco, led by Dr. Donald Abrams, conducted a randomized study with a control

---

[62] AA.VV., *Cannabidiol for treatment of refractory childhood epilepsies: Experience from a single tertiary epilepsy center in Slovenia*, in Epilepsy & Behavior Journal, April 2018.

[63] AA.VV., *Cannabinoid agonists showing Bunche inhibition as potential therapeutic agents for Alzheimer's disease*, in European Journal of Medicinal Chemistry, vol. 73, February 12, 2014.

[64] Maia Szalavitz, *How Cannabinoids May Slow Brain Aging*, Times, 29 ottobre2012.

[65] AA.VV., *Summary of evidence-based guideline: Complementary and alternative medicine in multiple sclerosis. Report of the Guideline Development Subcommittee of the American Academy of Neurology*, American Academy of Neurology, 24 marzo2014.

group. Through the daily monitoring of fifty-six patients, they established that "smoking cannabis effectively relieved chronic neuropathic pain from HIV-associated sensory neuropathy "[66].

The same results were also verified in pain therapy caused by other diseases, such as fibromyalgia[67]. Cannabinoid-based therapy for the treatment of spasms caused by this rheumatic form of disease has been recently included in health management guidelines in the Italian region Emilia-Romagna[68].

In general, several researchers have shown how cannabinoids are important modulators of the immune system and that therefore may play a role in the treatment of inflammatory chronic diseases. For example, CBD can be effective for the pain treatment rheumatoid arthritis[69].

Also promising are the results of the first research on another health concern, becoming more and more widespread: autism. A cannabis extract with high CBD content and low THC concentrations proved effective in relieving the symptoms of children suffering from autistic spectrum disorder. This is certified by the results of a recent American study, where it's stated that:

> *Following the cannabis treatment, behavioral outbreaks were much improved or very much improved (on the CGIC scale) in 61% of patients. The anxiety and communication problems were much or very much improved in 39% and 47% respectively. Disruptive behaviors, were improved by 29%*

---

[66] D. Abrams, *Cannabis for Treatment of HIV-Related Peripheral Neuropathy*, in Neurology, February 13, 2007.

[67] G. Habib, *Medical Cannabis for the Treatment of Fibromyalgia*, in Journal of Clinical Rheumatology, 14 February 2018.

[68] Kyriakoula Petropulacos, Linee di indirizzo regionali per la diagnosi e il trattamento della Fibromyalgia, Direzione generale Cura della persona, Salute e Welfare, Regione Emilia-Romagna, circolare n. 1. *1*, February 5, 2018.

[69] Mr. Malfait, *The no psychoactive cannabis constituent cannabidiol is an oral anti-arthritic therapeutic in murine collagen-induced arthritis*, Proceedings of the National Academy of Sciences, 10 March 2000.

The encouraging results have led researchers to conclude that:

> *This preliminary study supports the feasibility of CBD-based medical cannabis as a promising treatment option for refractory behavioral problems in children with ASD*[70].

CBD is also an important new frontier of study concerning Parkinson's disease. In 2014, a team of Brazilian researchers discovered how its use can improve well-being and the quality of life of patients suffering from this disease[71].

In patients with cancer, on the other hand, the use of Hemp derivatives is already a consolidated reality. It works to relieve sleep disorders, pain, weakness, nausea and lack of appetite. In various parts of the world oncologists today add it to the conventional treatments of chemo- and radiotherapy. But there is scientific evidence, reported in in-vitro studies and in guinea pigs, which posits that CBD and other cannabinoids even have the capability to kill cancer cells in different types of cancer, with no side effects on healthy ones. Positive results have already been obtained on lung cancer[72], on gliomas[73] and brain cancer[74], while a clinical study by the pharmaceutical company GW Pharmaceuticals, carried out with the administration of the aforementioned Sativex spray to twenty-one patients affected by an aggressive form of brain tumor, Glioblastoma Multiforme, showed a

---

[70] A. Aran, *Cannabidiol Based Medical Cannabis in Children with Autism. A Retrospective Feasibility Study*, American Academy of Neurology, 10 April 2018.

[71] MH. Chagas, *Effects of cannabidiol in the treatment of patients with Parkinson's disease: an exploratory double-blind trial*, in Journal of Psychopharmacology, 28 November 2014.

[72] M. Haustein, *Cannabinoids increase lung cancer cell lysis by lymphokine-activated killer cells via upregulation of ICAM-1*, in Biochemical Pharmacology, July 2014.

[73] K.A. Scott, *Enhancing the activity of cannabidiol and other cannabinoids in vitro through modifications to drug combinations and treatment schedules*, in Anticancer Research, October 2013.

[74] M. Solinas, *Cannabidiol, a non-psychoactive cannabinoid compound, inhibits proliferation and invasion in U87-MG and T98G glioma cells through a multitarget effect*, in Plos One, October 21, 2013.

survival rate of 83%, compared to the 53% among patients who did not have access to experimental cannabis-based treatments[75].

A true revolution in the consideration (at first) and use (afterward) of this plant is therefore taking place and as often happens in revolution, this began at a grassroots level, fueled by the courage of some sick people and their relatives who decided to make public their own stories of suffering and healing and have thus contributed to changing people's vision, increasingly aware that the movement against Hemp had been nothing more than a great deception.

A significant example in this regard is the one of little Mykayla, an Oregon resident who in 2012, at just seven years old, was discovered to have acute T-cell lymphoblastic leukemia: a rare and aggressive form of cancer that particularly affects children. A great quantity of lymphoblasts were removed from her chest with surgery, and then she began chemotherapy.

Initially the results were promising, but soon the cancer returned. On the day of the diagnosis, the level of lymphoblasts in the blood of Mykayla was 51%. Two days after starting chemotherapy it decreased, but only for a short time. It then returned to 31%.

Her parents, after coming to know a brave association in Portland, The Hemp and Cannabis Foundation, agreed to undergo an experimental treatment that combined chemotherapy with also the administration of cannabis oil. The day that Mykayla began the treatment, the level of lymphoblasts dropped to 5%, and after a few weeks there was no longer trace of it. The leukemia was officially in a state of remission.

The child's father then opened a blog: Brave Mykayla. Periodically, he updated it with data from the clinical analyses to which Mykayla was subjected, certifying that there was no resurgence of the lymph nodes, and he posted photos and videos in which the daughter finally appeared lively, smiling and awake. Everyone could see her jumping and dancing around the Christmas tree, drawing, and on her first day back at school.

---

[75] GW Pharmaceuticals, *A safety study of Sativex in combination with dose-intense temozolomide in patients with recurrent glioblastoma*, U.S. National Library of Medicine, June 2016.

She heals

Her story was told all over major American TV stations and the newspaper Vice produced a serial documentary entitled Stoned Kids to tell her story and that of other similar cases. New information and hopes reached many families who were living the same drama.

Criticism, however, came swiftly. "Some people accuse us saying that cannabis is inappropriate for children" the parents sadly published on the blog one day. "We say that it is the cancer to be inappropriate for children."

Unfortunately, too many people, including doctors and scholars, did not understand that cannabis was not just a drug. On the same blog, the little girl's parents explained:

> Mykayla never smokes Cannabis as we do. She instead uses Cannabis in many other forms such as, Whole Extract Cannabis Oil, Infused Agave Nectar, infused edibles, Holy anointing oil, and Raw Cannabis juicing. such as a natural juice not containing psychoactive substances (THC) normally present in a Cannabis flower, or in the form of oil in small, flavored capsule to mitigate their bitter taste. The little girl takes half a gram of Cannabis oil twice a day. All accompanied by a strict biological diet.

> Children undergoing anti-leukemia treatment have access to the same drugs as adults: antidepressants, analgesics, narcotics and nausea medications. With the Cannabis has only one biological and natural treatment rather than a great combination of drugs based on chemical. Cannabis has relieved nearly all of the horrid side-effects that we are warned about with each individual chemotherapy drug. Mykayla has experienced nausea, yes; though we are able to mitigate the nausea rapidly with crystallized ginger candies.

Currently, Mykayla's cancer is in complete remission. However, she is still required to undergo standard chemotherapy regimens for two more years; her diagnosis requires a three-year chemotherapy and radiation protocol in total.

Mykayla has needed the pharmaceutical anti-nausea medicine, Zofran, only a handful of times. She rarely, if ever, complains of pain anywhere; she hasn't experienced the chemo-associated neuropathy (foot-drop) that seemingly every child experiences when given Vincristine

Today Mykayla is a smiling thirteen-year-old teenager, and her leukemia has officially regressed for five years.

Her story really helped to break down a wall created by decades of misinformation in the United States. Within a few months, the number of parents who sought information about cannabis-based therapies for various pathologies multiplied; they started to lobby on doctors to get prescriptions and on politicians to get the legalization of the therapeutic use of Hemp.

It was a new beginning.

As a result of pressure from patient groups and anti-prohibitionist associations, more and more American states have organized referenda for the legalization of medical marijuana. And practically everywhere the "yes" vote has won at the polls. To date, only few out of fifty-two still don't recognize the possibility of treating yourself with cannabis for any kind of pathology.

Not bad for what had once been the homeland of prohibition!

But Hemp, which in the very century of prohibition had been the target of falsehoods, the subject of hoaxes and fake news spread to demonize it and justify its prohibition, among its many virtues must also have sense of humor: scientific research in fact is proving her effectiveness in treating those psychic disorders which, according to her detractors, she was the cause of.

For decades, in fact, we have been told that smoking weed leads to schizophrenia[76]. Instead – guess what – it has been proved that cannabidiol is an effective anti-psychotic, while a team of researchers

---

[76] C.D. Schubart, *Cannabidiol as a potential treatment for psychosis*, in European Neuropsychopharmacology, January 2014.

from the University of Medicine of São Paulo discovered that CBD can "reduce or block the symptoms of obsessive-compulsive disorder"[77].

On top of that, researchers at Washington State University, analyzing the data of almost twelve thousand cannabis intakes among patients, have shown how she has helped to reduce by 50% forms of depression and by 58% anxiety and stress[78]. This does not mean that cannabis cannot have side effects, especially on younger people. There have been several studies, some of which then denied, which have shown that a high use of cannabis with high levels of THC in adolescence has led to the onset of psychiatric pathologies, especially in predisposed subjects. There's also evidence linking this use to a decrease in memory.

A renowned case in Dunedin, New Zealand, seemed to show evidence that cannabis use in young people could lower IQ. Given the wide emphasis given to it by the press, some researchers cross-checked the data and came to the conclusion that so-called 'confusing factors' had not been considered. They were relevant to the economic status of families etc., data which in any scientific study must always be taken into account. These researchers explained that "even if it is exaggerated to say that the data have been falsified, the methodology is imperfect and the causal link is taken from premature data".

Although to date a unique truth has not been conclusively proven, surely cannabis consumption, until the brain is completely formed – i.e., around twenty-one years old – should not be taken lightly and should be avoided.

Having said that, it is clear that we are only at the beginning. Very soon new medical revolutions will take us by surprise. For example,

---

[77] M. Nardo, *Cannabidiol reverses the mCPP-induced increase in marble-burying behavior*, in Fundamental & Clinical Pharmacology, 3 October 2013.

[78] C. Cuttler, *A naturalistic examination of the perceived effects of cannabis on negative affect*, in Journal of Affective Disorders, August 2018.

cannabis-based therapies are being tested to cure addiction to nicotine[79], opioids[80] and to reduce brain damage caused by alcoholism[81]. When you hear someone say that "smoking joints leads to the use of heavier drugs" you can explain to them that actually the truth is the exact opposite. Cannabis is the antidote for heavy drugs.

Raise your hand if, before now, you had heard of these incredible studies in mainstream media. We are faced with the (re)discovery of a natural and revolutionary therapy, yet this research is not in the public domain. Fair information on the subject is completely lacking.

In Italy, cannabis-based treatments have theoretically been legal since 2008, when the then Minister of Health Livia Turco issued a special decree. However, actually getting them is a challenge that thousands of sick people have to undertake every day. First of all, you have to get a regular prescription. And it's far from simple. A normal doctor's prescription would be enough, but those willing to prescribe it are only a handful, from north to south of the peninsula. White coats are often uninformed or simply lacking the courage to do something entirely legal that still frightens.

For this reason, the sick often have to undertake true journeys of hope in search of a doctor willing to sign a simple prescription. This is also because Italian law relegates cannabinoid-based treatments to the status of "alternative medicines", in its pejorative sense, of therapies not entirely reliable. Cannabis can be prescribed by a doctor only when the ineffectiveness of all other medicines on the market has been ascertained and only for a very narrow list of pathologies. For the treatment of

---

[79] C.J. Morgan, *Cannabidiol reduces cigarette consumption in tobacco smokers: preliminary findings*, in Addictive Behaviors, September 2013.

[80] P. Lucas, *Medical cannabis access, use, and substitution for prescription opioids and other substances. A survey of authorized medical cannabis patients*, International Journal of Drug Policy, vol. 42, April 2017.

[81] D. J. Tickets, *Transdermal delivery of cannabidiol attenuates binge alcohol-induced neurodegeneration in a rodent model of an alcohol use disorder*, in Pharmacology Biochemistry and Behavior, October 2013.

oncological pain, for example, the law still prioritizes the prescriptions of opioid drugs. Nonsense.

Once the difficult stumbling block of the prescription has been overcome, the patient must then come to terms with regional laws. Another jungle. Diseases for which cannabis can be prescribed change from region to region, and so do the costs that the patient must bear. Some regions state that the treatment must be reimbursed by the Health Service, making them free for everyone. Others, on the other hand, leave patients to bear the costs. For many of them, this means being out of pocket of dozens of Euros every day. Often a patient needs three or four grams of medical cannabis per day. This amounts to more than three hundred Euro per month, as at the chemists it is sold for nine Euros per gram.

It's even worse for those who have to use cannabis derivatives like the Sativex. This spray costs about six hundred and fifty Euro per pack, comprised of four bottles, which on average is enough for just three weeks of therapy. It is a cost that many patients simply cannot afford.

Citizens are therefore forced by the State to renounce their right to treatment, or risk prison by courageously choosing to cultivate cannabis in their house. These are real injustices which for years have only been opposed by a handful of associations; small yet combative organizations such as *The Therapeutic Cannabis Association* (ACT), *Impatient Patients Cannabis* (PIC), the *Luca Cascioni Association* and *La PianTiAmo*. If things are slowly improving it is also – perhaps above all – thanks to them.

For those who can bear the cost or are lucky enough to live in a region that reimburses them, however, there is still one last obstacle to overcome. Cannabis for chemists, in fact, is produced directly in Italy, under a state monopoly. The health minister has authorized a single body – managed by the military – to cultivate two genetic varieties (FM1, containing 15% THC, and FM2, containing 6% THC and 9% CBD) provided by the Centre for Agricultural Research (CRA) of Rovigo. Production takes place at the Military Pharmaceutical Chemical Plant in Florence, in specially equipped greenhouses. The problem is that the Ministry has underestimated by far the amount needed to meet the needs of patients entitled to it. Only one hundred kilograms are available every year for chemists all over Italy, but this quantity is only enough for a few months, with the result of jeopardizing therapeutic continuity for thousands of citizens.

In some countries of the world, patients can grow the cannabis they need in their own homes. They can choose from many varieties developed by a more specialized seedbank. They can pick a variety based on the most useful genetics for their therapeutic needs. Or they can rely on medical centers who have the opportunity to buy on the market the most indicated type for each patient.

But even in this field Italy is incredibly behind, a hostage of a political class unable to do things right.

Chapter 13

LIFE IS A JOURNEY

As the green revolution spreads around the world and all the possible beneficial effects of cannabis in the therapeutic field are studied, for the first time in my life, I begin to think seriously about nutrition: I read books, I watch documentaries and I ask myself questions that I had never thought about before. If it is true that we are what we eat, I think it is right to devote time and attention to the matter.

One night in Milan a friend takes me to a place unknown to me, "a special place."

"Let's go in calmly, then follow me," he tells me. A typical phrase that usually foretells trouble.

It is a tiny place, around Corso Lodi, which from the outside is nothing special, with a small glass door full of stickers and a bright but faded sign. We walk through the door and hear some bells ring. Insides it's even smaller than what it might have seemed. Low lights, loud and unrecognizable music, a particular atmosphere, very relaxing: a good mix of style between an Irish pub and a Kathmandu lounge bar.

"Nice place!", I say to my friend.

He quickly greets the owner perched behind the counter, then I smile smugly.

"Follow me."

We cross the room heading to a door with the bathroom sign. "Where the hell is he taking me?" I think. He opens it and we enter a second room, a sort of improvised living-room with low sofas and cushions on the floor. The walls slapdash with boards and recycled material. It is a kind of extension of the bar, clearly illicit and very spartan, but quite welcoming and pleasant. Adding to the peculiarity of this exclusive space is the strong smell of Hashish in the air and the relaxed faces of the guests. The small groups of young people present sip warm herbal teas nonchalantly sharing fully loaded joints, well rolled, and lit. It seems like a kind of private club for hippies of the 2000s. In fact, my friend tells me, it is a "free zone" of the club, tolerated by everyone; police too, it seems.

"Wow, what a wonderful place!" is my first thought. "And how beautiful it would be to find similar places all over Italy, in every city!"

And I've been seeing a lot of cities. I zigzag between Milan, Vicenza, Belluno, Venice, Salento, Valencia, London. I move for work, for pleasure, for necessity. I need to move and at the same time I can work from anywhere. It's a rare privilege, I am aware of this; but what an effort! Especially on a psychological level. At times I feel saturated, too many inputs, too many stimuli. A revved-up engine. I have to slow down.

I put everything on standby and leave for a trek in the Himalayas with three friends. Walking in silence at the foot of the highest mountains of the world is therapeutic and regenerating. Here too I come across Hemp, that grows lush and spontaneous around high-altitude villages. It's a very light variety, completely harmless, and has been used by the locals for millennia for infusions and decoctions or as feed for animals. Seeing her free to grow without restrictions or prejudices makes me realize once more how ridiculous is her prohibition.

Sunrise at Annapurna Base Camp at 4,130 meters, with rarefied air and bitter cold, is an emotion of rare intensity. After two weeks away from everything and everyone, I bid Nepal farewell and return home. I am relaxed but at the same time increasingly intolerant of the city life. I vent it out in my diary.

The sky of Milan is fake: there are no more stars, not even clouds. It is an unnatural gray-yellow hood, an indescribable color. Even on a sunny day, the blue is faded. The city seems to be running but is actually still: cars everywhere, engines running, headlights on. Endless motionless queues. Behind the wheels people are increasingly similar to automats: hands firm on the steering wheel, head tilted forward, a fixed gaze, and brain on stand-by. The proof that these are humans is due to those who can't stay still, nervously smoking, screaming at mobile phones. Everyone with their own car, a car for every person, ten-hundred-thousand cars for ten-hundred-thousand people. I look at them and I don't see them smiling, ever. But not even complaining or puffing.

Total apathy. It's creepy. Outside the air is dense, it seems laying on the skin and it is not pleasant: I can almost smell it, an unhealthy stink. No bikes, pathways turned into parking lots, abandoned flower beds. This city is sick. God help us all.

In January 2011 in Cortina d'Ampezzo I meet by chance the famous journalist and TV presenter Bruno Vespa, strolling undisturbed through the streets of the Dolomite pearl. I try to stop him; presenting myself as a young independent journalist, I tell him that I'm disappointed by the way he handles his broadcast. He replicates that I should be ashamed, and that his broadcast is the only moderate voice on Italian television. When I challenge him, I accuse him of spreading disinformation and distracting Italians from the real problems of the country, at which point, he turns around and leaves.

But I recorded it all with my phone and put it on the net. This is what every citizen should do when he meets similar characters, anything but asking for a selfie or an autograph; especially if you are a journalist. Piero Ricca[82] docet!

After thirty-one issues, *Dolce Vita* has a new logo. The first one was drawn by me, and now after five years, is inappropriate, sloppy, amateur. This time I decide to rely on the web, and, through an appropriate website, I organize a graphic contest where I have to choose among more than three hundred proposals that come from all over the globe. The new brand is effective, impactful, simple, and modern. It appears for the first time in the February 2011 issue.

The magazine continues to grow, in every aspect: we got to seventy-two pages, the contents are better written, the distribution reaches an increasing number of stores, and also the web presence increases.

---

[82] Intrepid journalist and blogger, who became known for his videos in which he criticized politicians and public figures.

Hemp, an incredible story

Everything's going well.

But *Dolce Vita* is not my only focus. I carry out other projects, always concerning communication and journalism, out of pure interest and personal growth. Among them, I like to go in search of characters that I think are interesting, special people that I think are worth meeting and interviewing. So, thanks to some contacts of my father, I get an hour with Reinhold Messner. He welcomes me at Castel Firmiano in Bolzano for a 360-degree interview. It is a meeting that, together with the reading of his books, changes my life. Many know him for his enterprises in the mountains – unrepeatable and inhumane – or for some commercial endeavors, but there's actually more, much more. Messner is a giant, a philosopher, a man who turned his life into a work of art.

I publish a video recording of our chat on the web. Somebody, months after that, will call it "the best interview ever done to the king of the eight thousand". I'm proud of it.

Besides him, I have the honor of meeting and listening to other great characters of our times, from Silvano Agosti to Mauro Corona, from Mario Attombri to Fausto De Stefani, Lucio Dalla, Eugenio Finardi, Luigi Di Maio, Serge Latouche. Very different people, some known to the general public others not as much, but each with something precious to tell.

About Finardi: rereading some parts of the lyrics of his *Legalizzatela* (Legalize it) of 1979 makes us understand how brave and forward-thinking he was:

> *No one wants to take a side, no one wants to face the situation, but there is only one solution. You don't need the police, send them away, there is already too much hypocrisy. Legalize it! You can't put it on the same level as those who use needles or smoke a joint with those who smuggle tons of heroin to undermine a generation, they do not deserve neither the same penalty nor the same acquittal. Legalize it!*

My hunger for travelling is not satiated and at the end of May I leave for an almost mystical itinerary. I want to cycle the Camino de Santiago, this time solo, and mix with the pilgrims, try to understand their faith, pedal until I can't take it anymore. I take two books with me: a light version of the Bible and *The flower of evil*, the autobiography of Renato Vallanzasca. The sacred and the profane. They seem perfect for the occasion, and they will be; even though, to be honest, the busy life of Renato is more compelling, and especially more realistic.

Nine hundred and fifty kilometers traveled in just under two weeks, from Saint Jean Pied de Port, in the south of France, in the Pyrenees, to as far as Santiago de Compostela, in northwestern Spain.

A new summer arrives and watching the documentary *Earthlings* convinces me that I no longer want to be part of a system that I consider obscene, unfair, wrong, unhealthy. My consistency, my sensitivity and my intelligence impose on me a drastic change in eating habits, among other things. So, I stop eating meat and I'm starting to drastically reduce other animal proteins as well. From now on I intend to join the fight, with the means at my disposal, to give my small contribution for changing the unacceptable mechanisms of the carnivorous industry, or at least to stop being its accomplice.

Even the editorial line of *Dolce Vita*, avoiding any extremism, is affected by this novelty.

Changes extend to other aspects of my life. I leave Milan for good and move back to my native village, in the mountains, together with Valentina, my girlfriend.

At that time in Val di Susa, the Battle of the No-Tav rages. They are fighting against crazy civil work that the government is trying to impose with force.

I follow events from afar and would go in person, but I cannot. Now is the time to take it easy, because on 10 March 2012 I become a father. Sebastian is born and it is the beginning of a fantastic new journey. Life inevitably slows down and I'm happy about it. Do I feel ready? Will I ever be? Has anyone ever been? I'll do my best, as always, more than ever.

I decide to be de-baptized. "I've got nothing against god," Woody Allen said. "It's his Fan Club I can't stand."

I don't want to be part of the Catholic church, in any way. I basically do not share anything about what it does and how it does it. I'm actually disgusted by its "representatives", who often have opposite visions to the ones of its followers. That's why I finally decide to give shape to that idea that had been going around in my head for quite some time. De-baptizing is very simple, simpler than you can imagine, and there are more and more people doing it, thousands every year only in Italy. You just need to fill out a form – available on the website of the Union of Atheist and Rationalist Agnostics (UAAR) – and send it to the parish where you have been baptized, which is required by law to answer within a fortnight confirming the operation.

I do it and I feel free!

At the end of the year, I fly to Africa with two friends, I climb – with inhuman fatigue – Kilimanjaro at 5,895 meters and I dive into the immense parks of Tanzania. I am astounded by so much beauty and my deep gratitude goes to those people who have defended and preserved it.

In the forty-fourth issue of January 2013, we finally publish the news of the imminent legalization of cannabis for recreational purposes in the states of Colorado and Washington. Uruguay too is moving towards making this step. The green revolution has really begun and above all it is difficult to stop. In Italy we are still behind, but, at least, we start to see a glimpse of light at the end of the tunnel.

At the same time in Racale, Puglia, the first courageous attempt of an Italian Cannabis Social Club takes place. Andrea and Lucia, respectively Secretary and President of the association La PianTiAmo, decide to make public their battle for the freedom of treatment with cannabis, especially to help other people in their same situation who need it. We immediately support them in this crusade.

At the 2013 general election, for the first time, the 5 Stars Movement participates, obtaining over 25% of votes and resulting in the most voted party in Italy. It's an incredible achievement that surprises and destabilizes traditional parties. In total, there are one hundred and sixty-three M5S elected MPs, including deputy Federico D'Incà, of the province of Belluno, who contacts me a few weeks later and offers me a role as his communications assistant. It is an important commitment that requires responsibility. I take a few days to reflect on it, then accept the assignment. I enter for the first time the palaces of power in Rome and come in contact with a world of which I don't know much, if anything. I am both fascinated and disgusted at the same time. In any case it is an interesting, formative and intense experience. The congressman, who does not want to be called that but prefers "elected citizen", is an incredible Stakhanovite, a person of rare honesty and determination. Working for and alongside him is an honor.

In the spring we publish an article about Bitcoin in *Dolce Vita*. It is the beginning of the cryptocurrency revolution, a phenomenon not much spoken about by mass media, but which is strongly opposed by traditional finance.

At the beginning of the summer together with Mario Catania – professional journalist and, for a year now, our collaborator – I open two new web portals specific to therapeutic cannabis and industrial Hemp. They are side projects to the magazine, which aim to reach an audience interested in these two sectors, where the novelties are at the order of the day. CannabisTerapeutica.info aims to inform as many people as possible on the medical uses of the plant, telling stories, studies, events, to provide the necessary tools to stimulate in everyone their own opinion on the matter. CanapaIndustriale.it, on the other hand, wants to update on the thousand opportunities for industrial and craft use offered by the plant.

After years without dedicated trade fairs in Italy, the first edition of *Indica Sativa Trade* in Fermo, Marche, takes place. It's a new beginning, the merit of which goes to the organizers, who with determination and courage give life to an event of quality and depth. *Dolce Vita* is media partner of the fair and significantly contributes to its success.

I turn thirty and look at myself in the mirror: everything is going great, I have to keep on going like this, I don't have time to stop and celebrate now, I'll do it next year.

1 August 2013 brings the first final conviction for tax fraud to Silvio Berlusconi. From that day it is legitimate to call him a criminal.

Meanwhile, for the first time, we print on FSC paper (Forest Stewardship Council), a mark that certifies the origin of raw material from properly managed forests.

Hemp, an incredible story

In autumn I leave for a trip to Japan and discover a wonderful country, full of history, culture and contradictions. For me it is new lifeblood, and I go home after a couple of weeks recharged and enthusiastic.

In October, walking around Montecitorio, I see a few steps away from me no less than Carlo Giovanardi surrounded by a series of arse-kissers, lackeys or similar. I can't do anything but stop him. I hand over a copy of *Dolce Vita* and introduce myself. As he, disgusted, browses through the pages, I immediately declare our position, namely that of convinced anti-prohibitionists, after which I ask him, in a civilized and calm way, if he realizes how much damage he has done with his shameful law. I tell him that I speak on behalf of thousands of people whose lives he has ruined and that I could tell him countless stories of suicides, of people and families on the brink because of him. He ducks my sentences with the defense, reiterating that he saved so many people with his law and that scientists have told him that "joints burn the brain."

Before I leave, I ask him for his phone number for a possible debate, although I know that there won't ever be one. The inevitable anti-prohibitionist wave and scientific evidence are overwhelming him and soon his law will be just a sad memory.

Chapter 14

THE NEW ERA

At the beginning of the new millennium, while Italy was still immersed in the repressive swamp created by the Fini-Giovanardi law, things began to change overseas.

In 2010 in Uruguay a very particular man became president. His expression of a peaceful and charismatic elder could not completely hide a face marked by the years lived as a revolutionary, with a rifle on his shoulder, and the long detention suffered under dictatorship. His name was José Alberto Mojica, but everyone called him Pepe. From the stage he talked about social justice and criticism of consumerism, he harangued the crowd inviting them to reflect on things that too often are given for granted:

> Life is a miracle, being alive is a miracle. And we
> cannot live oppressed by the market that obliges us to buy,
> again and again. Also, because we don't pay with money
> but with the time of our lives that it took us to earn them.

Splendid concepts of great wisdom; but, beyond these, Mojica became famous first of all for a revolutionary law that his government became the first in the world to approve on December 10, 2013: the one that legalized cannabis.

While at every latitude consumers continued to suffer jail time and repression, and had only mafia and criminal as a way to restock, three million and two hundred thousand Uruguayans could buy cannabis in pharmacies for less than one euro per gram. They could grow it freely in their garden, or join non-profit consumers clubs who, independently, produced and distributed weed to its members.

> We do not defend marijuana, but we believe that
> drug trafficking is much more dangerous. We apply this
> principle: if you want to change a situation you cannot
> keep on acting the same way. We've been thinking about
> repressing it for decades and every year the situation has

> *worsened. Now we've decided to try to embark on a new journey, and if by chance this new road will prove to be successful, we will have done something that will help all mankind[83].*

So Mujica continued, who with these arguments had tried to also convince the UN General Assembly; but from Turtle Bay, in response, he received the threat of sanctions for violating the Convention on drugs stating that each State must commit itself to fight against drug diffusion and consumption.

The warning obviously did not stop him: much more was needed to frighten a man who, for defending his ideals, had spent nine years in solitary confinement inside an underground well.

However, no one from the UN had the courage to follow through on the threats, because by now the failure of prohibition was before everyone's eyes; and, while Uruguayan law followed its own parliamentary process, increasingly authoritative voices rose to ask for a radical reform of the Convention.

Among these emerged the report of the Global Commission for Drugs Policies, signed by prominent figures such as former Secretary-General of the United Nations Kofi Annan and former Presidents of two of the countries that had paid the highest price for the war on drugs, the Colombian César Gaviria and the Mexican Ernesto Zedillo. The report expressed neat and clear concepts:

> *The global war on drugs has failed, with devastating consequences for individuals and societies around the world. Fifty years after the initiation of the UN Single Convention on Narcotic Drugs, and 40 years after President Nixon launched the US government's war on drugs, fundamental reforms in national and global drug control policies are urgently needed.*

It goes as far as encouraging

---

[83] Excerpt of the speech given by José "Pepe" Mujica during the presentation of his book Happiness in Power, held in Rome on 28 May 2015.

> *experimentation by governments with models of legal regulation of drugs to undermine the power of organized crime and safeguard the health and security of their citizens. This recommendation applies especially to cannabis, but we also encourage other experiments in decriminalization and legal regulation that can accomplish these objectives and provide models for others*[84].

In Europe, the report went almost unnoticed, but in the Americas, it had the effect of telluric shock. The presidents of several South American states issued statements in which they declared the will to abandon prohibition. Uruguay was no longer alone and the race towards marijuana legalization spread into the homeland of prohibition itself, those United States of America where everything had begun almost a century before and where federal law continued to consider cannabis as a drug to be banned and repressed, like heroin, according to the classification of narcotics imposed back in the days of Harry Anslinger.

Starting with the west coast states, the wind of reform began to blow stronger and stronger. As early as November 2012, voters in Colorado and Washington were called to the polls to decide whether to legalize cannabis in a referendum where they opted for 'yes'. Within a few years they were followed by Alaska, Washington, D.C., Oregon, California, Nevada, Massachusetts and Maine. Everywhere that citizens were called to express themselves, they showed themselves to be tired of prohibition and its collateral damage, and of wanting an end to the criminalization of Hemp.

In these states the cultivation of the Plant for personal consumption was allowed and the first dispensaries opened up, shops where all citizens over the age of 18 could legally buy marijuana and her derived products. The social and economic consequences of legalization were closely monitored and analyzed by governments and independent studies.

It did not take long before the data silenced every prophecy of misfortune spread by defenders of the prohibitionist status quo.

---

[84] *Global Commission on Drug Policy, War on drugs,* June 2011.

In defiance of the "passing theory", in states where cannabis had become legal, opioid overdose deaths began again to decrease, reversing year-long trends that had seen them constantly increasing[85].

In order to oppose the referendum, the adverse lobbies sought to instill terror with the usual safety concerns, announcing uncontrolled increases in car accidents caused by high motorists, murders, rapes, thefts, robberies and any other possible social crime. But instead, none of this happened.

And what about the alarm that, in order to scare parents, suggested devastating increases in marijuana consumption among young people? Here, too, the exact opposite occurred, perhaps because reefer, in becoming legal, lost that charm of the forbidden thing that always attracted adolescents; or maybe because in schools, at the same time, they started informative campaigns finally free from prejudice and false myths. Hard to point down the merits, the fact is that both in Colorado and in the State of Washington Cannabis use among under-eighteens fell consistently, data which is even more resounding because it was in contrast with those of the rest of the nation[86].

In short, it took only a few months of legalization to empirically disprove all the false paradigms that prohibition had spread for almost a century. In addition, the legal market took away power and resources from the hands of the organized crime bringing them under government control. Washington State, for example, within a few years' time collected from legal cannabis US$281 million dollars in taxes, while in Colorado it was US$205 million[87]. These funds were then used to fund

---

[85] M.D. Livingston et al., *Recreational Cannabis Legalization and Opioid-Related in Colorado, 2000-2015*, in American Journal of Public Health, n. 11, November 2017.

[86] Between 2013 and 2015, the rate of Cannabis users among U.S. citizens between the ages of twelve and seventeen fell by an average of 0.42% (from 13.28% to 12.86%), while in Colorado it fell by 2.46% and in the State of Washington by 1.92%. Statistics available at the internet address: http://samhda.s3-us-gov-west-1.amazonaws.com/s3fs-public/field-uploads/2k15StateFiles/NSDUHsaeShortTermCHG2015.htm

[87] Colorado Department of Revenue, *Marijuana Tax Data*. www.colorado.gov/pacific/revenue/colorado-marijuana-tax-data

information and prevention campaigns as well as projects of social value, such as the award of scholarships for the poorest students, the construction of new social housing, and increases in funding for public schools.

In addition, in the United States one hundred and sixty-five thousand people found work in the legal marijuana industry, in different types of activities more or less specialized: growers, selectors, food producers of cannabinoids or other derivatives, traders, transporters, quality controllers, researchers and much more.

And alongside these direct benefits we must not forget the indirect, produced by the dismantling of a repressive system of prohibition. In the first year of legalization in Washington, arrests for crimes related to the consumption or minor dealing of light drugs collapsed from over five thousand the previous year to just one hundred and twelve (98% less)[88] while in Colorado they halved[89].

This led to a series of good news for the United States: people's lives were no longer ruined for the simple consumption of cannabis, the pressure on the justice system were eased because courts were no longer paralyzed by hundreds of unnecessary criminal proceedings, and police departments spared means and men who could be employed for the persecution of real crimes.

Yep, this happened in the United States.

What about in Italy?

---

[88] AA.VV., *Court Filings for Adult Marijuana Possession Plummet*, ACLU Washington, 19 March 2014.

[89] AA.VV., *Marijuana Legalization in Colorado. A Report Pursuant to Senate Bill13-283*, Colorado Department of Public Safety, Marzo 2016.

Chapter 15

HEMP WON

In Italy, 2014 began with a bang: on 12 February, the Fini-Giovanardi law was declared unconstitutional.

Thousands of lives ruined by a law that went against the Constitution. And we knew it, we said it!

The world is going through great changes and *Dolce Vita* with it: cannabis and all its uses – recreational, botanical, therapeutic and industrial – are still the heart of the magazine, but around her, over time, we've built a mosaic of columns that narrate a different world, alternative, often ignored or even censored.

In March, we launch the new website of *Dolce Vita*, a daily updated portal that we aim to quickly make the online reference point of the industry and a new entry in the counter-information landscape.

A few months later, the magazine's fifty-second issue is published and for the first time we reach a hundred pages. The work increases, the staff expands, and things get more and more serious.

The entire sector is growing: shops open up all over Italy and two new trade shows are announced, first in Naples and then in Rome.

Nevertheless, the offensive of the usual prohibitionists and bigots continues. The media occasionally spreads hoaxes against cannabis, but finally we can replicate and start publishing – both on paper and online – precise denials with references to scientific studies, facts, statistics and incontrovertible data.

Our audience has also grown, and now we reach hundreds of thousands of people. And every day, more and more people start following. We are read by doctors, politicians, entrepreneurs, lawyers and our target audience expand from 18-year-olds to fathers of families, a group that is diverse and varied. Our work is becoming more and more important.

Hemp, an incredible story

I'm doing well, I feel fulfilled, but at the same time far away from the final goal. My ambition does not wane; indeed, it continues to grow and is fed by success. I have also to keep at bay my imagination and inventiveness, every day new projects and challenges cross my mind. I dream of founding an eco-village on the Marche hills, I dream of a new trip in South America, I dream of explaining to the world that there we are not too many, but that we consume too much.

In the summer issue we talk about our idea of Europe.

> *I would like a Europe completely different from the current one. I would like a Europe capable of being an example for the rest of the world and not, on the contrary, able only to pursue models that I consider insane, such as the American one. With our culture and our history we should be a lighthouse, not a taillight. I would like a Europe capable of being heard on international politics and impose, at least on its territory, the choices of its inhabitants. I'd like a Europe capable of promoting its specific characteristics avoiding homologating each nation following the myth of globalization. A Europe less focused on money and more on personal happiness. No more austerity at all costs and open to alternative new solutions: they exist, the time has come to take them into account and have the courage to implement them. I would like a Europe with more eco-villages and fewer eco-monsters, with more Hemp and less chemistry, with mare great parks and less great construction works. A Europe that is less frenzied, but more capable of looking further away.*

At the end of September, I go to Taranto to see the foundry Ilva, to have a live impression of it, to try to understand. Its sight entering the city is impressive, like a medieval fortress. A multitude of smokestacks. It's impossible to understand how such a situation can still exist in 2014. It is a factory that, according to some studies, emits 90% of all the dioxin produced in Italy. It has killed and continues to kill people every day, causing incalculable and permanent damage to the environment... But it guarantees jobs! Thousands of jobs. Thus, nothing gets done. Thus, nobody talks. Thus, people die. All of this is – objectively - monstrous.

Hemp won

At the same time in Bisceglie – still in Puglia, but on the opposite side of the coast – I have the opportunity to visit the construction site of the largest European housing complex built of lime and Hemp. Amazing! This plant manages to amaze me every day. This plant – I'm personally more and more convinced, as was the good Jack Herer, can really save our planet.

Winter arrives and it's time to travel again. It's time to go in Peru, Bolivia and Argentina. A fantastic trip, between Machu Picchu and Lake Titicaca, between the immense salt ocean of the *Salar de Uyuni* and the Bolivian highlands, to end up in Buenos Aires. Oxygen for the soul!

On 20 April 2015, *L'Erba voglio, legalize it is right and convenient*, a public meeting promoted by Pippo Civati, a formerly leading member of the Democrats, is staged in Milan. I am invited to speak, but my speech, which is still available in full on YouTube, is certainly not what the organizers expect. I point out, in fact, that in the last fifteen years I've seen too many of events like that one, but none has then led to any change. Actually, many of those members who now argue the need for a new law were in the house when the Fini-Giovanardi law was passed and, even if they did not vote in favor, they certainly did not oppose it with enough emphasis. Legalizing cannabis is correct, of course, I have always supported it, but without comparing it to alcohol and tobacco which, although legal and unlike Hemp, take tens of thousands of lives per year; and without forgetting that in addition to the therapeutic and the recreational uses, the plant has immense potential in the industrial and energy field.

The audience in the room appreciates what I say, much more than the organizers and the attending politicians, including Daniele Farina, Benedetto Della Vedova and other exponents of the Italian left.

At the beginning of the summer, a new parliamentary intergroup called *Legal Cannabis* finds the support of more than two hundred members of the lower house and seventy of the upper one, from various parties. This is the first time in Italian history that a pro-legalization law is presented by so many supporters.

We are happy about it, of course, but at the same time we are very skeptical. We follow closely all the developments and give much prominence to the thing, but "unless we see (results) we will not believe".

Sixty thousand signatures are collected in support of this bill in a very short time, thanks to an initiative led by our friend Luca Marola, anti-prohibitionist, militant of the Radicals and among the first entrepreneurs of the sector in Italy.

That summer, *Dolce Vita* turns ten years old. The first issue was presented to the *Rototom Sunsplash* in July 2005. It seems like a lifetime ago and one day ago, it depends on the point of view.

In the meantime, *Rototom*, which has become one of the most important reggae festivals in the world, moved (with reason) to Spain, because Italy did not deserve it and did not know how to manage it. We, on the other hand, remained here and became a magazine that was (almost) serious, some would say prominent: we definitely carved out our space in the panorama of alternative and independent publishing. And in small steps, we grew.

In the world, after almost a century of persecution, we are experiencing the rediscovery of Hemp in all her forms. It was inevitable, but to have the privilege to be able to see it with my own eyes was not so obvious. In the *Bel Paese*, on the other hand, we are in slight contrast with the rest of the world, as usual. And therefore, despite bipartisan slogans that promised imminent legalization, a clinic for addiction to cannabis is opened and the witch-hunt against consumers, patients included, continues.

Personally, I am convinced that as things stand the best solution is self-production: three plants each and that is it. In my opinion weed should be as free as chamomile and you should be able to sell, buy, exchange, give, cultivate, eat, drink, smoke and do anything you want with it. But the world is not ready for this yet – much less Italy – and so, for the time being, let us try to regulate self-production, which would already be a good result.

The Milan Expo, dedicated to feeding the planet in a healthy and sustainable way, opens its doors. It is a shame that among the sponsors we find Coca-Cola and Mc Donald's. It's insane! We propose a more realistic and coherent alternative with a new issue dedicated to Hemp as a superfood.

And then it happens that, ten years after that first fair, I meet my former boss again, that of the Dutch magazine for whom I had worked for a year, the same one that fired me with two lines in an email without explanation. In these interceding years he has yielded the ownership of his magazines and founded a seedbank. He comes looking for me, interested in an advertising space for his new entrepreneurial project: "Matteo, it is clear that in Italy your magazine is number one. I want my ad in your magazine".

A bit of water has passed under the bridge and I am convinced that if he could go back in time, he wouldn't have fired me with such ease. While he signs the advertising contract, I'm filled with a small but fulfilling satisfaction.

At the beginning of 2016, the Facebook page for *Dolce Vita* reaches one hundred thousand subscribers.

On 10 April, Howard Marks, better known as Mr. Nice, leaves this world and moves on to a better life. Marco Pannella follows him closely, on 19 May. I wonder about the parties up there, with those two together!

In the summer in Forlì comes the first edition of the *Hemp Festival*, an event in which we immediately believe and which we support with pleasure. Other important projects are taking place in Saracinesco, in the province of Rome, and in half of Italy. A startup is born in Sicily that offers Hemp bioplastic filaments for 3D printers. The first 100% Hemp shoes made in Italy came from Marche. CBD revolutionized the seed and seedbanks market, with new oils and extracts arriving. It grows - everything grows.

Chatting with a friend and colleague in the Italian cannabusiness, we agree with a little melancholy that maybe the golden age of this sector has already passed: the exasperated race to open new stores, the cynicism and opportunism for their own sake in the start-up of new activities, the unhealthy competition between small companies and in general, the craving to make money (and more money) with cannabis are unfortunately compromising a world that, though perhaps naive, we thought different and healthier than others. It is certain though that we do not want and cannot resign ourselves to the fact that even this sacred plant, with all its derivatives and all the items necessary to cultivate it and then consume it, become an ordinary commodity. For this reason, I issue a warning on the next issue by writing in my column:

> *Let's all look a little further than the receipt at the end of the day, the invoice or salary at the end of the month: Hemp deserves more.*

On the regional news in Piedmont they speak of THC as "a new drug with tremendous effects" spreading among teenagers. We cannot take it in silence! We move to counterattack and with our loyal lawyer, Carlo Alberto Zaina, file a complaint with to the Telecommunications Authority. Six months after, indeed, the Order of Journalists of Piedmont sanctions the two colleagues who wrote the story.

It is the first time in Italy (and perhaps also in Europe and beyond), that misinformation on Hemp is sanctioned. *Dolce Vita* is making history.

In the July issue we publish an exclusive interview with George Jung, known as Boston George, the protagonist of the movie Blow, played by Johnny Depp. We also release a video online, in which George holds our magazine and advises everyone to read it.

I turn thirty-three and I'm incredibly happy. It is in this moment that I decide to write a book about Hemp and my story with her. Or, at the very least, what I can tell about it without putting one, namely myself, in trouble. Everyone has skeletons in their own closet; in mine, in addition to skeletons, at some points were also fragrant plants (which are unfortunately still forbidden). I think it's a story worth putting in writing.

It's autumn - travelling time. I've had a trip in mind for many years, and now I finally realize it: it is the Trans-Siberian, from St. Petersburg to Vladivostok. Onboard a train that does not exceed eighty kilometers per hour, through immense Russia. Once we arrive at our destination, I would do anything to stay longer on that cozy "spaceship."

I return to Italy and in November the draft law for the regulation of the industrial Hemp supply chain is approved in the Senate, unanimously. A good step forward!

Unfortunately, however, 2017 starts with bad news. It's 2 January, when suddenly, at the age of forty-two, Franco Loja, co-founder of Green House Seeds Co. and internationally renowned strain researcher, dies. A great lover and supporter of cannabis, he dedicated his life to this plant. This is how he spoke of her:

> *Cannabis is my passion, my bread, my home. I feel that it's my duty to make sure that this amazing plant is preserved and enjoyed by all. I will be a smoker, a farmer, a breeder and a strain hunter for life.*

In past years we cooperated many times for work related issues and, although there were no direct collaborative relationships with the company he worked for, we kept the possibility open. There was mutual esteem and great respect. He was a very willing person, humble and with a great heart. The world of Hemp thus lost one of its protagonists.

In March we publish on the *Dolce Vita* website an article that drives much interest from the title "Smoking Canapone is fashionable in Switzerland, and the thing is driving the police crazy". Canapone is cannabis without psychoactive effects, with very low THC percentages and higher values of CBD, therefore perfectly legal. On social media, the most popular comment by users is: "why don't we do the same in Italy?!".

In Greece, the inaugural edition of *Dolce Vita Hellas* is published. It's produced between Thessaloniki and Athens by a young girl who a year before had expressed to me the desire to devote herself to the Hellenic edition of the magazine, the first to deal with the subject in Greece. And so, the " *Dolce Vita family*" made another step towards conquering the Mediterranean.

On 1 May 2017, Stella is born, my princess, my second child. I feel like the luckiest man on earth.

On 11 May, we publish on our website, before anyone else in Italy, an absolute preview: an article on Cannabis Light. It's the beginning of a new phenomenon that will soon revolutionize, for better or worse, the whole industry.

I decide that it's time for the magazine to take another step forward, and I invest in logistics and events, increasing the number of copies and their distribution, advancing content and printing. Thanks to an intuition from our editor-in-chief Enrica Cappello, we finally start using 100% recycled paper and from now on we report the data of an Eco-computer showing all the resources saved in each issue[90]. *Dolce Vita* grows to a hundred- and twenty-four-pages in total.

The seventy-first issue in August 2017 comes out with an unequivocal title: *You can't stop her anymore! Hemp won.*

You bigots, wands, conformists, puritans but above all prohibitionists, oil lords and those of big pharma and finally politicians hostile to change, get a grip: Hemp won, you can't stop her anymore. Just accept it and step aside.

You won't do it, we know that well, and that's why we're going to keep on going with our battles against your moral and legal laws, your infinite speculations, your monopolies and exploitation of all kinds. They will collapse one day, crumbling like a wall falling apart. And in the end, of you, there will be nothing but a faded sad memory.

You've been able to fool the world for long, too long, basing your thesis on a series of filthy lies and falsehoods. That's enough, your time is up. It's time for free Hemp, in all its forms and for all its uses.

I know well that it will be necessary to be patient for a bit longer, it will take a few years to allow politics to adapt to the will and needs of society. Nothing new: politics – especially in Italy – always arrives late, but in any case – it arrives.

In the meantime, however, we must begin to tackle seriously the use of this plant, to understand how to exploit it at her best, without

---

[90] Choosing Eural Premium 100% green paper for the realization of the magazine, compared to a virgin fiber paper, *Dolce Vita* actively contributed to the environmental protection saving: 3,715 kg of waste, equivalent to the average output of a family of three in three years; 15,451 Kw/h of energy, equal to the consumption of a family of three in four years; 833 kg of CO2, equal to gases emitted by fourteen cars on the Milan-Rome route; 116,351 liters of water, equal to the consumption of a family of three in two hundred and twenty-two days; 6,039 Kg of wood, equal to fifty-four saved trees. Data generated by the Two Emme Packs eco-computer, LabeliaCounseil evaluation, Bilan Carbon method(c).

abusing her, without taking advantage of her, but respecting the sacrality of this gift of Mother Nature. This is our new challenge.

The one against cannabis detractors has already been won.

Chapter 16

A GREEN FUTURE

Closely related to our challenge of figuring out how to use cannabis at its best, there is a much bigger one of global importance.

The traditional media talk about it superficially and laconically, between local news reports and the football transfer market, yet more and more alarming health reports have been circulating about our planet.

For example, in the middle of the Pacific Ocean, between California and Hawaii, due to a strange combination of sea currents, a huge island of waste has generated: it's called the *Great Pacific Garbage Patch*. It is - in fact - an island 99% composed of plastic, micro-sized residuals no longer identifiable, fishing nets, packaging, bottles, glasses, straws, cotton-buds, stockings and much more. It is the floating landfill of our single-use civilization. Today it is estimated that the Patch extends for at least 1.6 million square kilometers - more than five times the size of Italy. Five times the landmass of Italy, entirely covered with plastic. It is impossible even to imagine it, at least for me.

Four similar islands, although a little smaller, can be found in other areas of our seas, and no one can bet on the fact that there are some more yet to be discovered. In the meantime, cases of cetaceans found dead with their stomachs full of plastic bags swallowed after having mistaken them for octopus or other prey are on the rise.

This plastic becomes part of the food circle and reaches humans, sometimes indirectly when we eat fish that ate plastic, and at other times directly, through water bottles exposed for too long in the sun, by cups melted by hot coffee or tea, or food packaging produced at low cost. Without realizing it, the western man ate so much plastic that he's now marching inexorably towards mass sterility.

It's all scientifically proven, even if you can't hear much of it in the news.

Chemical compounds called phthalates are used to produce plastics. Once taken, they cause effects like those of estrogen hormones, leading to the feminization of male newborns, and to disorders in the formation of the testicles. The result is that within forty years fertility has halved[91].

In the same period, the oil economy has brought civilization one step away from the ecological and social chasm, decisively contributing to global warming, making the air of our cities irrespirable and relegating every person on earth who happened to have the luck of living on hydrocarbon-rich soil to the role of victim of the arrogance of multinationals.

It is no coincidence that all this happened in the century of Prohibition. We saw how Hemp could have avoided it, if given the chance. But the news that interests us more, having quickly touched on the story of this war that never appeared in history books, is that perhaps we still have time to reverse the course. And more and more there are those who are trying to do so today with courage and determination. All thanks to her, Mrs. Cannabis.

Waste from the processing of Hemp fibers is almost 80% from cellulose, a raw material necessary to produce bioplastic. To make a comparison, wood produces less than 50%, and while cotton does reach levels like those of Hemp, it has a yield per square meter cultivated considerably lower, as well as slower growing times and greater environmental impact. Hemp is therefore the most efficient cultivation for eco-sustainable plastic, also because among natural fibers is the one able to guarantee greater elasticity – thus resistance – to the final product.

This is already happening. Throughout the world, dozens of realities are producing plastic from Hemp. In China, there are innovative companies such as Hemp Plastic and Shanghai Yuezhan Chemicals that produce Hemp plastic granules in different versions with scratch-proof quality, resistant to heat and ultraviolet rays. All over the world – including in Italy – Hemp cellulose is among the most sought-after ingredients for the production of bioplastic objects through the use of 3D

---

[91] AA.VV., *Temporal trends in sperm count: a systematic review and meta-regression analysis*, in Human Reproduction Update, vol. 23, Issue 6, 1 November 2017.

printers. Hemp plastic is thus becoming more and more successful in the cutting-edge production of materials for furniture, packaging and toys, thanks to the advantage of being completely non-toxic, unlike conventional plastic.

One of the most important manufacturers of automotive components in the world, the French Faurecia, a titan of seventeen billion-dollars turnover per year, produces doors, steering wheels and body parts using Hemp fiber. Thanks to the fibers of the magic plant, mixed with traditional alloys and with other natural products such as corn starch, its components weigh 40% less than in the past and are 30% stronger than common metal car bodies, all while reducing the amount of CO_2 emissions during the manufacturing process. You probably don't know this, but Hemp parts are already present in many models of Audi, BMW, Ford, Chrysler, Mercedes, Lotus and Honda.

A Florida-based company, Renew Sports Cars, has recently put on prototypes of a car whose body is 100% made of Hemp fiber on the market. For now, there are three different versions, including a turbo powered one. They offer performance in line with the best sport cars and, thanks to the Hemp and corn bioethanol power supply, pollute even less than an electric car[92].

"Why decimate forests that have formed over the centuries, and rely on mines that will take centuries to reform, if we can obtain equivalent products by growing Hemp?"

This is the question, as simple as ambitious and visionary, that Henry Ford asked himself before the fury of prohibitions took over. With almost a century of delay, his dream is finally becoming a reality. In order to power cars without having to drill the planet there is a need not only for biodiesel, but also electric energy. And even in this case, Hemp is at the center of research.

Researchers at the University of Alberta, Canada, are studying super-condensers, a new type of battery that within a few years could revolutionize electric cars powering systems thanks to the use of the best

---

[92] *Hemp behind the wheel: from America an ecological car made of Hemp*, www.canapaindustriale.it

materials for energy conduction. The goal is to produce batteries with the capacity, charging speed, durability and production costs capable of finally making electric cars completely competitive with those powered by hydrocarbons.

At the base of the super-condensers are nano-sheets, electrodes made of thin foil with great carrying capacity and energy storage properties. By using graphene as a material for the construction of nano-sheets it has been possible to make this type of battery preferable to lithium ones, as far as charging time and life span are concerned – with a life cycle of more than ten thousand charges. However, two problems remain: capacity retention, which is too low, and production costs, which are still too high.

Canadian researchers have therefore taken new paths, trying to use new natural materials with high electrical conductivity, instead of graphene. They tried with peat, then with eggshells, then with banana peels. Results were encouraging, but not enough. Then they made a further attempt. Using industrial Hemp production waste, they extracted the crystalline cellulose that makes up 70% of its fiber, then cooked it, keeping it under pressure for twenty-four hours at a temperature of 180 degrees Celsius, treated with potassium hydroxide and heated it to a temperature of 800 degrees. The first nanosheets made entirely of Hemp were created. The result? A capacity to discharge 49 kilowatts of power per kilogram of material - almost three times standard commercial electrodes, which stop at 17 kilowatts per kilo. This results in shorter charging times and better car performance.

Hemp foils have also proved excellent in ensuring one of the essential advantages of super condensers: the capability to use the car's braking to recharge. According to scholars at the University of Alberta, once mass produced, Hemp super condensers could have paltry costs, up to a thousand times lower than those with graphene, which is priced at about two thousand dollars per gram[93].

---

[93] AA.VV., *Interconnected Carbon Nanosheets Derived from Hemp for Ultrafast Supercapacitors with High Energy*, in ACS Nano, vol. 7, 2013.

A green future

To see first-hand how the future will look, it is not always necessary to embark on long intercontinental journeys. I've realized this in June 2016, when an editor of *Dolce Vita* went to San Giovanni in Persiceto, just outside Bologna, to meet with Mr. Franchini, who for three years had been living in the first house built from Hemp and lime in Italy.

"I am amazed by the feelings of living in this house. I was used to normal houses, to heat loss and living with the feeling of moisture on the skin, especially living in the Po Valley. Now instead I enter the house and it's a beautiful feeling."

Mr. Franchini was really excited about his nonconformist choice. The works lasted for three years, from 2009 to 2012, during which time, a devastating earthquake struck Emilia. Several nearby dwellings had been damaged, but the structure of Hemp and lime did not have any issue, absorbing the strong shock. According to studies, buildings manufactured with this technology are completely earthquake-proof and even in the case of heavy shocks, over seven degrees on the Richter scale, they guarantee high chances of survival thanks to the fact that the walls would shatter rather than collapse.

But the benefits of cannabis-based green building don't end here.

A building made with this technique allows a reduction in energy consumption, because thanks to the natural ability to retain heat, it provides a cool environment in summer and a warmer one in winter. The quality of the plant in retaining carbon dioxide translates into better air quality inside the house and in a large benefit for the environment.

These factors can give a decisive contribution to improving the construction sector which, according to estimates, is currently responsible for 30% of global CO_2 emissions. Builders have been realizing this more and more over time. Hemp houses are now spreading all over the world and for once, Italy is part of the vanguard.

This mistreated plant is also being used for projects of high social value. One such example is in Nepal where, following the terrible earthquake on 25 April 2015 which caused the deaths of more than eight thousand people and destroyed many houses, Hemp was placed at the center of reconstruction. Today in the capital, Kathmandu, the collapsed parts of the old hospital were re-built with bricks in Hemp and straw, while new homes for citizens of the Dhanush district, in the south-east of the country, are built using the same technology.

These are just a few examples, because the ways in which she may improve our planet – if we only give her the chance to do it – are truly innumerable.

At an industrial level through Hemp, it is possible to produce paper of excellent quality without deforestation. You can make fabrics, clothes, cosmetics and natural detergents. It can be used in food production for bread, pasta, oil and many other foods with excellent nutraceutical properties thanks to the natural balance of Omega 3 and Omega 6. And every day researchers discover new possible uses of her. From the creation of antibacterial clothes, capable of preventing the proliferation of staph infections, to military and high-tech equipment for the capability of her fibers to withstand infrared rays.

While waiting for all this to turn from a vision of the future to daily reality, cannabis – as if all this wasn't enough – is already showing that she can carry the cross of environmental damage caused by her killers. Among her infinite qualities in fact, she is also a bio accumulator. It means she is able to absorb the chemicals present in the soil and hold them within her, therefore proving to be a fundamental agent in soil Phyto-depuration practices.

Among the elements that Hemp can assimilate are heavy metals and even radioactive substances. It is a quality that we have already known since the beginning of this millennium, when she was successfully employed in experiments on land contaminated by the Chernobyl disaster. A 2003 study found that the presence of Hemp on a polluted field led in a few months to a decrease, compared to the initial concentration, of thirty-fold for zinc, thirty-five-fold for copper, ten for nickel, six for lead, twelve for chromium and three for cadmium[94].

But it's only been in the last few years that we're starting to get serious. In Taranto, Hemp fields have been planted to reclaim land

---

[94] A. Piotrowska-Cyplik, *Phytoextraction of heavy metals by Hemp during anaerobic sewage sludge management in the non-industrial sites*, in Polish Journal of Environmental Studies, vol. 7, 2003.

polluted by Ilva's industrial activity. The same is being done in Sulcis, in Sardinia, and in other places in the world. And where Hemp is planted to clean up land from disasters caused by the most harmful industries, she also helps to revive the economy.

Nature, when she designed this incredible plant, really outdid herself, no kidding. Cannabis traps substances absorbed in the roots, leaves and flowers, but not into the fiber[95]. This allows the use of the same plants sown for purification to also produce paper or tissue without any risk of contamination.

All this progress has been made in no time, mainly over the last five years, without any public investment, if not for those from a handful of enlightened research centers, and almost always starting from small startups rich in ideas but certainly not in resources. This factor is not to be neglected, in the technological research world, where the possibility of investing large sums makes a difference in almost every case.

In 1937, we saw specialized American journals hailing cannabis as the 'billion-dollar harvest', capable of saving forests and providing raw material for the production of over twenty-five thousand different articles. Then, whether planned or not, the main effect of prohibition was certainly not to "free the planet from drugs", as the masters of the world ambitiously declared, but rather to deprive the planet of the possibility of a development in harmony with the environment, handing it over to the destructive power of plastic and oil.

After the long era of prohibition obscurantism, everything is changing with an unexpected and overwhelming speed. In April 2016, the UN approved a document guaranteeing member states "sufficient flexibility to design and implement drug policies according to their own priorities and needs." It may not seem like much, but in the very measured language of diplomacy it is half of a revolution. It means that governments that deem it appropriate may decide to change their legislation on light drugs without risking any sanctions. The wave of change has then got as far as the palace in Turtle Bay. The same palace

---

[95]L. Arru, S. Rognoni, M. Baroncini, P. M. Bonatti, P. Perata, *Copper localization in Cannabis sativa L. grown in a copper-rich solution*, Euphytica, 2004.

that Harry Jacob Anslinger managed to turn into the austere control tower from where orders of war on Hemp were given.

In this way, countries like Jamaica and South Africa have approved rules that decriminalize the cultivation of cannabis for personal consumption. Without counting states – from Zambia to Colombia, passing through much of Europe and Latin America – who have loosened their laws and legalized therapeutic use for the ill.

Finally, the most recent chapter of this story was written in June 2018, when Canada became the first member state of the G7 to legalize all uses of cannabis. And you can bet on it: it is just the beginning of a green future.

Hemp revolution is therefore a silent one, but inexorable. Medicine, the construction industry, the environment: once again she is ready to take center-stage in history.

Will the world finally have the courage not to stop her?

Chapter 17

DAD, WHAT IS HEMP?

Master Terzani will forgive me from up there if I dare to steal five lines of his posthumous masterpiece - *The end is my beginning*. After all it has been one of the books that has influenced me most. A passage in particular:

> *I have invented this life of mine, certainly not a hundred years ago, but the day before yesterday. Everyone can do it, it just takes courage, determination, and a meaning that is not the little one of career and money; be it the meaning that you are part of this wonderful thing that's here all around us. I would like my message to be a tribute to diversity, to the possibility of being what you want to be. It's doable, it's doable for everyone. Making a life, a life. A real life, a life where you are yourself. A life where you recognize yourself.*

It is also thanks to these words that I have found the courage to invent mine. And if I had to go back, I would not change one bit.

I was lucky, it is true, but luck must be intercepted, fed, valued. Otherwise, it passes in front of us without us even noticing.

My greatest luck was discovering this incredible plant, having the curiosity to study her, to understand her and to defend her. I believe she saved me. I owe her much and I hope I have done her honor and justice with these pages.

"And now Matteo, do you still smoke joints?"

Tell the truth, you were wondering it, right?

"Very, very rarely" is the answer. And if it happens it's in particular circumstances, strictly dedicated to smoking – preferably Pakistani Chitral Kush – and just a few puffs. To make it short it can be said that I do not smoke any more, for a long time now. That's the way it is today, and as for tomorrow, who knows?

Maybe in the future I will return to using cannabis as a stimulant or relaxant. On the other hand, I'm using it more and more often as food, medicine, and cloth ware.

Summer 2018. I'm sunbathing lying on a beach in Croatia. Valentina – my partner and mother of my children – plays with Stella a few steps away from me. Sebastian runs, dives and swims in blue indigo water. He's six years old and full of energy. He comes out of the water and throws himself on me. We tickle each other a little bit, laugh hard, and then we stop, hugging each other and face up to the sky. We look at infinity. There's a moment of silence. And then out of the blue he asks me:

"Dad, what is Hemp?"

Afterword

You know my past from Johnny Depp's performance in the movie "Blow". I ask now to speak to you with a wealth of extremes in the hope that it will fuel the legalization movement to end the schizophrenia that reefer causes madness. The right people and circumstances are already here and will show up on time.

Weed is from the earth... God put it here for you and me. The legalization movement is growing into a worldwide monster and shall not fail. Ironically, the Jamestown Colony in 1619 passed a law forcing the settlers to grow cannabis. Hemp was a mainstream cash crop used to make rope, fabrics and ship sails. How far we have fallen!

In 2012, police arrested one U.S. citizen in every 42 for pot related offences. The vast majority -87% - met the criteria for possession, not intent to sell.

I've been involved in drug culture my entire adult life. I grew rich by smuggling. I speak with the experience of having seen it all. To continue arresting people is draconian and evil.

I urge you to never let the few that are bad take away the good of the many. Let's join as one and end this strange dance of myth and reality. Truth haunts the air. Think it, believe it, manifest it. The dream is the weapon. We will take down the greed that feeds the fear. It's a magical moment, a liberation is afoot.

In conclusion, I would like to thank Matteo for allowing me to speak through his book, emphasizing the madness of prohibition as it relates to the cannabis industry.

Being one of the largest drug dealers in history, I can say without a doubt that if weed was legal when I was involved that I would have never involved myself in the world of smuggling. Prohibition is a friend of the drug trade and legalization their worst enemy.

Today, with this great book by Matteo, we add an important piece to the history and culture of Hemp, another small step towards the legalization of this sacred plant.

Hemp, an incredible story

George Jung
aka Boston George

Glossary

Apical: the primary growing point located at the top (Apex) of the plant. Some cannabis growers decide to trim it with various techniques to obtain one of more of it.

Bad-trip: term used to describe a particularly negative and traumatizing experience with hallucinogens.

Inside out: A type of rolling for eliminating excess paper. It can be made with or without the glue side of the paper.

BHO (Butane hash oil): Substance made by blasting marijuana flowers with butane which may have THC content that exceeds 80%.

Bong: Tool for smoking cannabis or hashish. It's made from a bowl and a stem, and it filters and cools down the smoke through water.

Breeder: Cannabis genetics selector.

Cannabinoids: Chemical compounds contained in the cannabis plant. The most well-known is THC, which is also the only one with psychoactive effects, and which can get you high. More than 100 compounds have been identified though, and many of them have medical and therapeutic properties.

Cannabis Social Club: associations born in Spain which allow cannabis consumption within the clubs created by members who cultivate it according to their needs.

The L: A type of rolling that involves the placement of two papers perpendicular to each other, so to make a longer joint.

Dutch Tulip: A rolling method using a variable number of papers and a filter. The name comes from the final result, which recalls precisely the shape of the flower.

CBC: Cannabichromene is a cannabinoid that seems to be the one carrying anti-inflammatory and anti-viral properties, and may contribute to amplify the analgesic effects of Cannabis. It does have not psychotropic properties.

CBD: Cannabidiol is a metabolite of Cannabis sativa. It has relaxing, anticonvulsant, antioxidant, anti-inflammatory effects. It helps sleeping and alleviates anxiety and panic attacks. It has also turned out to be able to reduce intraocular pressure and is a promising atypical antipsychotic.

Charas: resin of Indian origin obtained from cannabis through the technique called *finger hash*, which is the rubbing of the flowering-buds on the palms of the hands.

Cyloom: Tool aimed at inhaling the fumes of combusted materials. Progenitor of the pipe, it consists of a long conical pipe, more or less decorated on the outside, with a conical filtering stone on its inside.

Chocolate: nickname of a particular variety of hashish.

Coffee-shop: premises in the Netherlands authorized by the State to sell small quantities of light drugs to consumers.

Dab: concentrated form of Cannabis obtained by extraction. It usually has high content of THC.

Munchies: sudden hunger that often follows cannabis consumption. Known reaction to all regular consumers.

Pot: colloquial synonym of hashish.

Ganja: synonym of marijuana, from the Hindi term used to identify the medicinal product prepared with cannabis flowers.

Grow box: cabinets or boxes for the indoor cultivation of cannabis.

Grow shop: offline or online store, specialized in items for cannabis cultivation.

Hydroculture or Hydroponics cultivation: off-soil cultivation technique in which the earth is replaced by an inert substrate and the plant is irrigated with a solution of water and mineral salts. It allows monitored productions, both from a qualitative and hygienic-sanitary point of view, throughout the whole year.

Joint: spinel, made of marijuana or hashish.

LSD: diethylamide-25 of lysergic acid, is one of the most powerful psychedelics substances known. It causes amplifications of the senses, emotions and distortions of perception of reality.

Orange Bud: Well-known high quality cannabis variety.

Pusher: drug dealer.

Raphael Mechoulam: researcher considered the father of research on Cannabinoids. In addition to discovering THC and identifying for the first time the structure of the CBD, he has produced more than 200 scientific publications on cannabis.

Salvia Divinorum: psychoactive plant, natural hallucinogenic.

Seedbank: Cannabis seed bank that collects and studies genetic characteristics varieties of the plant.

Endocannabinoid system: The human body has specific binding sites for cannabinoids on the surface of many cell types and our organism produces different endocannabinoids, similar to those contained in cannabis, that bind to cannabinoid receptors (CB), activating them. CB1 and CB2 receptors and endocannabinoids make up the endogenous cannabinoid system.

SOG and SCROG: these are two techniques designed to maximize yields in small cultivation spaces, optimizing the light coverage on plants.

Strain: variety or type of different genetics of cannabis.

Terpene: substance contained in cannabis and other plants which, in addition to giving odors and flavors to the flowering-bud, protects the plant and acts in synergy with cannabinoids and other substances.

THC: delta-9-tetrahydrocannabinol, is the active ingredient of cannabis responsible for its psychoactive effects. It was isolated and discovered in 1964 by Israeli scientist Raphael Mechoulam.

Trichomes: the main sites for the synthesis and accumulation of secondary metabolites are of the tiny structures and called glandular trichomes. In addition to cannabinoids, most monoterpenes and sesquiterpenes produced by the plant are largely located within these structures. Trichomes are the elements of the plant that are most important from the pharmacological point of view.

Vaporizer: tool to intake cannabis or her extracts without combustion. The principle is that of vaporization that allows to increase the intake, and without harmful substances, the active ingredients of the plant.

BIBLIOGRAPHY

- *Hemp as a medicine*, Grotenhermen F., Huppertz R., Leoncavallo Libri, 1999.
- *Christopher Columbus' ships*, Ciano C., Gay F., Polygraphic Institute e Zecca dello Stato, 1992.
- *The writings of George Washington*, Washington G., Worthington Chauncey Ford, 1989.
- *The Emperor wears no clothes*, Herer J., Ah Ha Publishing, 1985.
- *Hemp*, Bröckers M., Herer J., Parole di Cotone Edizioni, 1999.
- *Cannabis in medical practice*, Mathre M., Mc Farland, 1997.
- *Marijuana in medicine: past, present and future*, Mikuriya T., Calif Med, 1969.
- *Marijuana reconsidered*, Grinspoon L., Harvard University Press, 1971.
- *Marijuana: the first 12000 years*, Abel E., Plenum Press, 1980.
- *The Great Book of Hemp*, Rowan Robinson, Bear & Co., 1996.
- *Drugs and minority oppression*, J. Helmer, Seabury Press, 1975.
- *Canapa, Cannabis, marijuana*, J. Herer, M. Brockers, Parole di Cotone Edizioni,1991.
- *Legalizing Marijuana: Drug Policy Reform and Prohibition Politics*, R.J. Gerber, Greenwood Press, 2004.
- *The Traffic in Narcotics*, H.J. Anslinger, W.F. Tompkins, Funk & Wagnalls Company, 1953.
- *Marijuana Law in a Nutshell*, M. Osbeck, H. Bromberg, West Academic Publishing, 2017.
- *Fight against drugs: collateral damage*, F. Corleone, A. Magara, Edizioni Polistampa, 2010.
- *Copper localization in Cannabis sativa L. grown in a copper-rich solution*, L. Arru, S. Rognoni, M. Baroncini, P.M. Bonatti, P. Perata, Euphytica, 2004.
- *Marijuana reconsidered*, Grinspoon L., Harvard University Press, 1971.

- *Vanity Fair*
- *Soft Secret*
- *Times*
- *Mechanical Engineering Magazine*
- *Popular Mechanics Magazine*
- *The San Francisco Examiner*
- *Medical and Surgical Journal*
- *The Military Surgeon• Janesville Daily Gazette*
- *Journal of the American Medical Association*
- *Epilepsy & Behavior Journal*
- *European Journal of Medicinal Chemistry*
- *Neurology*
- *Journal of Clinical Rheumatology*
- *Journal of Psychopharmacology*
- *Biochemical Pharmacology*
- *Plos One*
- *U.S. National Library of Medicine*
- *European Neuropsychopharmacology*
- *Fundamental & Clinical Pharmacology*
- *Journal of Affective Disorders*
- *Addictive Behaviors*
- *International Journal of Drug Policy*
- *Pharmacology Biochemistry and Behavior*
- *ACS Nano*
- *Polish Journal of Environmental Studies*
- www.canapaindustriale.it
- www.dolcevitaonline.it

www.ingramcontent.com/pod-product-compliance
Lightning Source LLC
Chambersburg PA
CBHW072005290426
44109CB00018B/2144